Life Circles

Life Circles

A Self-help Book to Improve Your
Relationships, Marriage, and Life

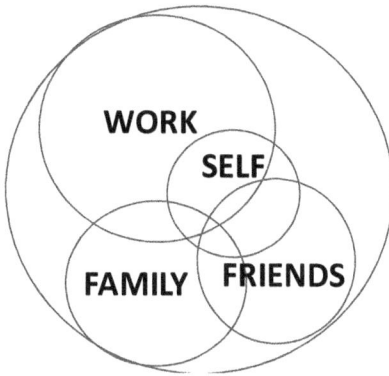

Robert O. Lewis

FOREWORD BY
Jeanne Vinson

RESOURCE *Publications* · Eugene, Oregon

LIFE CIRCLES
A Self-help Book to Improve Your Relationships, Marriage, and Life

Resource Publications
An Imprint of Wipf and Stock Publishers
199 W. 8th Ave., Suite 3
Eugene, OR 97401

www.wipfandstock.com

PAPERBACK ISBN: 978-1-5326-8588-0
HARDCOVER ISBN: 978-1-5326-8589-7
EBOOK ISBN: 978-1-5326-8590-3

Manufactured in the U.S.A.

Dedicated to
Deborah and Lyla

Contents

List of Illustrations

Foreword

WHEN I FIRST READ *Life Circles*, I was impressed with the simplicity of Lewis's approach to helping people analyze their human relationships with each other and God with strong hints on what to do to improve their lives and especially their marriages. In my practice as Licensed Professional Counselor, but more importantly as a Christian Counselor, I find people that have no idea how to get started in evaluating their own situations or trying to improve their relationships. Read deeply as Lewis describes Faith, Family and Friends, in that order. *Life Circles* addresses people of all ages and situations with pragmatic ideas on how to create balance by improving their lives and the lives of those around them. His beautifully written, easy to read, personal experiences woven throughout the book provide a stage on which you can find yourself and see how his mistakes, as well as accomplishments, will encourage everyone who finds their life in a mess. I encourage you to take *Life Circles* to heart. It can help you weather the hard times life throws at us all from time to time.

Jeanne Vinson MS. LPC, Christian Counselor

Preface

I STOPPED AND STARTED this book several times over the past twenty years and now find myself in a position where I have learned a lot more about myself in the interim based on events that I never thought I would experience. Some were great and some were quite painful, but I count all these things as blessings because they have made me a more loving, understanding, and faithful person. Regardless of your spirituality, I believe that you must involve God through prayer to guide you in making the important decisions you and your family face every day and in every way.

I want everyone who reads this book to picture themselves in some of the situations I describe. Some are anecdotal and funny while some are sad, and several are stories told me by others who wanted to contribute to this book to help others who find themselves in similar situations. I mention them here to let you know you are not alone. Millions of people are where you are in your life. Some will move forward, and some will slide back. Some will never improve their situations, and some will find a way to achieve better balance and become much more positive and happier people. This book will help you find your way and put you in a position to better control the forces that affect your life.

Acknowledgements

I WISH TO THANK my daughters Lyla and Deborah who encouraged me to finish writing this book. They are both my strength and inspiration.

I wish to thank several people who read early drafts and made suggestions and contributions: Emily, David, and Jeanne, as well as others who shared their stories with me and shall remain nameless.

My sister Judy who did the first complete and thorough edit for me.

My good friend Lynne who did the final editing and formatting.

I am very grateful to you all.

Introduction

THIS IS A SELF-HELP book that is targeted at young adults, married couples, and divorcees of all age groups who have a nagging feeling that something vital is missing in their lives or, in worst case, are seeking help uncovering the causes before their lives completely unravel. The book makes the readers take an introspective look at their lives by making them do some self-evaluations at the beginning of the book and again at the end. It offers just-in-time guidance in cases where the reader has a divorce or remarriage pending to help them avoid another mistake. It is also helpful in repairing neglected marriages and those challenged by combined families when divorcees remarry. The book exposes life forces that many people do not realize exist or chose to ignore, and it helps you bring your life and that of your family under the protection of God and the Holy Spirit. It focuses on and helps you rebalance your main four Life Circles and helps you have enough time for all the good things in life you need. The book includes vignettes of the author's life and shared stories both good and bad by others whose lives have been shared with him to help the readers evaluate their own situations and decision making.

One of the shocking statistics uncovered in writing this book is how many older empty nesters are divorcing. This group is rising significantly just when they should be more able financially to enjoy some of the finer things in life together. This should be the time to travel and doing all the things you postponed for years waiting for the kids to leave. I have some sage advice for this group. Start doing your bucket list before it is too late.

The best news comes in the last two chapters on how you can improve your life and that of your spouse and children by fully embracing the rewards God has provided for us here on earth and in the hereafter. I encourage you not to be a lukewarm participant in your walk with God. Become a strong believer and willing participant, and you will be rewarded forever.

1

Finding Out Where You Are

FINDING OUT WHERE YOU are tells you a lot about yourself. The challenge of this chapter is to help you discover where you are in the relationships you have with the main elements and forces in your life. Most of us can readily identify four major components of our daily lives: Family, Friends, Work, and Self. We are going to be using circles I call Life Circles to define these major components in terms of their importance to us and how much time you spend in each circle. If you spend about the same amount of your life with two of those components, then those two circles are the same size.

It is very helpful if you begin this analysis of yourself with a pen or pencil and draw the circles the size you believe they are in relationship to each other. You may want to finish reading the chapter first and then come back to make several attempts before doing the final ones you will need to save, perhaps folded up in the book.

Let's start with Work and Family circles. Most people work 8 to 10 hours per day including commuting time, so a bit over one-third of our Monday through Friday time is spent at work. This can be considered the baseline for the rest of the circles we are going to draw. Our job is important, especially if we are the sole breadwinner of the family, so try to estimate what size your Family circle is compared to your Work circle. You can allow for time on the weekends with family, so those two circles should be about the same size. Sleep time is when you are in bed and bathing, etc. and is deducted from the total hours but not factored into this exercise. Now go ahead and draw your Work and Family circles. These are just examples shown in Figure 1 below.

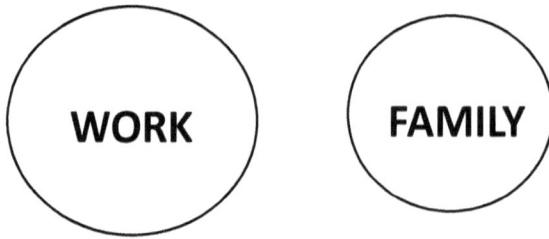

Figure 1. Example Life Circles

Now let's take a few minutes to see where all the time in one week goes: There are 168 hours in a week and we already know we spend at least 45 hours working and in transit and in some places, it takes a lot longer. In this book, we'll use 45 hours as the Work baseline. Use the pen and paper to collect your actuals. You need to record them for analysis later. We sleep an average of 8 hours x 7 days, which takes another 56 hours away from available time to do other things and we need more time for dressing, bathing, and all those things that take off another 7 hours a week at least.

Thus, most families are left with about 60 hours, and if we take half those hours for Family time at 30 hours including meals, that leaves just 30 hours (less than 5 hours a day) for us to do all the other things we may want or need to do, or if you work longer hours, you will have even less than 30 available hours a week.

One extremely important "need to do" thing is weekly worship, which for Christians is going to church, and it is my family's habit to join with others for the noon meal every Sunday. When we got married, my wife informed me that we will always go out for lunch after church and that tradition continues to this day. It is a nice reason to dine with friends and share our week with them. Our children also picked up the habit and do this, too, on most Sundays. It's all about fellowship and keeping friendships energized in a totally relaxed atmosphere.

Managing all the "other things we want or need to do" has a severe physical limitation. If you have a couple of children, they have a lot of demands on these 30 hours, some of which are in the

Family circle, and some are not. Sometimes when the breadwinner comes home, things are in chaos because children often have competing places the parents are required to take them, and schedule conflicts mess up routines and mealtimes together. Balancing home life today can be a tedious business.

Forward planning helps somewhat, but can't solve all the things that occur every week that produce conflicts and competition for whatever time is available. Just remember: people today find they often run out of time to do all the things they really *need* to do. For example, take doctor appointments where waiting times are sometimes hours long; and to make matters much worse, many families today, especially the younger ones, have both parents working. Factor out those hours. It turns into a scheduling mess, often requiring husband and wife to divide their efforts to get everything done.

The pace of life today is much faster than it was 40 or 50 years ago, and a lot of it results from overly organized things for people to do. Parents are made to feel guilty if their kids aren't into multiple sports, clubs, after school activities, etc. You name it, it's on everyone's agenda today. More on that later. It will keep coming up because it is a never-ending problem.

Next draw a Friends circle. How large is it in comparison to your Family circle? In my example shown in Figure, I start them out about the same size. Do you play golf, some sport like tennis perhaps, go on long bike rides, work out at the gym, have a hobby that takes a lot of your time and involves friends? Factor in whatever you can and see if you need to borrow hours from the Family circle. The other trick is that if you share some of these activities with the family, they can be overlapped synergistically, which saves a lot of hours you would otherwise have to allocate to each circle separately.

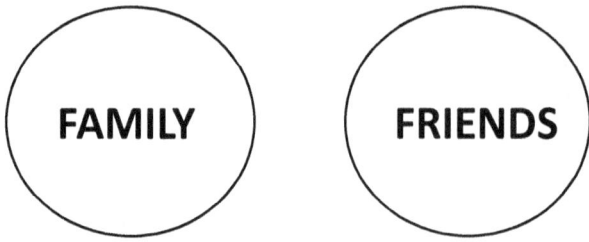

Figure 2. Typical Family and Friends Life Circles

The more you share your life circles, the better and the more efficient your activities become. You might think of it as a form of multitasking, but I like to call it just simple sharing. God likes to see people interacting and sharing.

Remember, you typically have only 30 hours each for the last two circles. Chances are, you may need a few hours from somewhere because you start running out of time. So, you borrow it from wherever you can, which is usually Family time. I want you to be very honest with yourself and only change the size of the Family circle if it is required. Now see how Family and Friends circles compare. A one-week sample of your time distribution may have to be based on the average time each month you devote to each circle. Another adjustment you may have to make during this process is be honest about the time you are gone from home for work and be sure to include your commuting time, which is becoming a major source of lost hours. In larger cities today, congestion can easily cost you ten hours a week or more, so it adversely affects how much time you have available for everything else. It has become the bane of suburban living in all large metro areas.

In making these estimates, you may say to yourself, I need some time to meditate to forget about work or problems I am having with relationships, or whatever may be bothering you at that moment. I advise you not to meditate excessively while driving in heavy traffic, but a solitary commute will give you time by yourself to think about issues and problems you are facing in the days ahead. Hopefully, you can use some of this time constructively. I know someone who runs a company and deliberately lives at least 35–40 miles from work and uses his daily commute for problem solving. Do what works for you.

Think back over the past month or two and be as careful and honest with yourself as possible. If your Friends circle is significantly larger than the Family circle, you may be heading for problems in the future. Now to make matters even more complicated, add in the hours for the Self circle from the 60 total available hours or whatever you came up with in your calculation. It is the "all about me" circle. If you do a lot of things without family or friends, then the Self circle can grow larger than the Friends circle. A risk you may run if this occurs is that you become too self-centered, a loner, an introvert, and you may lose friends as a result. That defined my father, God bless his soul.

I am reminded of an old song whose lyrics suggested that people who need to be with other people are lucky, happy people. We were made by God to be with other people; we are social beings. From the beginning, God made us to have relationships, which in turn teaches us how to get along well with others and builds character. Remember, it often takes several people working together to do nice things for people who have big needs.

When we look at many people's behavior today, it is appalling that so many play computer and cell phone games by themselves for hours on end to be continuously entertained by such trivial stimuli. It is far better to be with friends exchanging ideas and discussing what is going on in the world around them and with each other, or better yet, doing something constructive. The problem with self-gratification is that it never teaches social skills, it never helps the person mature into someone who cares deeply about others and the significant issues of this world that count.

God wants us to grow up to be mature adults willing to help make this world a better place to live and to prepare us for the life hereafter, and you won't get there with a video game. Do something to help people instead of being a slug. While I am on this subject, going off by yourself to meditate has some value, but you might be better off taking a walk with a friend and talking as you go. People need to have a purpose in their lives that involves other people, but sometimes it is very difficult as I found out.

About 20 years ago, I was in St Louis working on a proposal and in the cafeteria by myself eating lunch and when I finished, I had noticed two men both sitting with their Bibles open, so I got up and went over to the table on an impulse, introduced myself, and asked if I could join them and they said, "Yes we mind, this is a private study." I said, "Sorry I bothered you" and went off literally quite shocked, thinking, "Some Christians you are!" I never tried that again.

Another time, I invited a friend to a breakfast at our church. Afterward in the parking lot, he told me not to invite him to anything else. I had said nothing to him to try to recruit him to come to our church. So, the devil throws up walls in front of us, sometimes, and makes it hard to be a disciple. But don't give up; just keep on trying even when you get embarrassed in the process.

We all need to find things to do that help others, and in so doing, we please God and feel so much better inside that we gave freely what we have so others could benefit. After all, whatever we have belongs to God anyway, and we're just passing through, so use it wisely.

If you spend some of that time in the Friends circle with others building a ramp for a person in a wheelchair, or repairing a poor person's house, or taking food to a person who is laid up, you please God. You must realize that if you are blessed with much, in turn, much is expected from you. In the parable of the rich young ruler, he asked Jesus, "Good teacher, what shall I do that I may inherit eternal life? And Jesus responded favorably to his question and said you know the commandments and the young man responded that he had always kept them, so Jesus loved him and in conclusion said, you only lack one thing, go your way, sell whatever you have and give to the poor, and you will have treasure in heaven; and come take up the cross, and follow Me! But the young ruler was sad at this word, and went away sorrowful, for he had great possessions." Mark 10:21–22. Jesus knew the man valued his possessions more than his salvation. We do not ever want to make that mistake.

It is not a sin or evil to acquire wealth as long as it is the byproduct of good honest work and uses the talents that God gave you; in fact, it can be quite the contrary. Think of all the good things you can do with it. I will have more to say about this subject throughout the book. God loves a cheerful giver, and moreover, he created us to become more and more like Jesus as we live here on earth and serve the downtrodden, poor, and those in need.

When considering the Self circle, Jesus went off to pray and be alone frequently because he felt compelled to talk to his father to make sure he remained true to his mission and to regain his strength. Remember, it drained his energy when he performed miracles and spoke to crowds, so he was not being reclusive, but rather he was being re-energized to face temptations of the devil and the awesome responsibilities of self-sacrifice that lay ahead to save all who believed and put their trust in him.

How do your circles compare to those in Figure 3? Be sure to save your original circles. Don't let them get away; we will use them again.

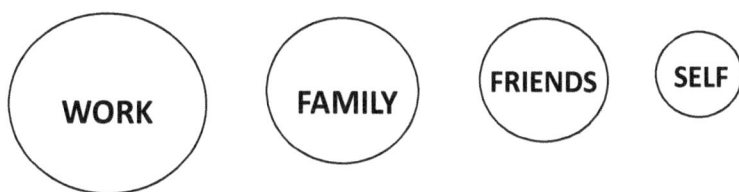

Figure 3. Example of Anyone's Life Circles

The first Remedial Step is to achieve better balance with your family life. Balance is not necessarily a 50/50 split. If your family needs the lion's share of the available time, so be it. It is more important to celebrate a family birthday than it is a round of golf. Men tend to be worse than women in this area. Men tend to rationalize away a lot of the negative aspects of a situation, often through substitution, thinking a gift or a dozen roses or box of candy will make everything right. Those things are important at the right time and place but not as a replacement for your time.

Your time is golden, it is the richest thing you have to give away, so spend it wisely and don't squander it on worthless, petty indulgences. Individual situations need to be included in this analysis. Once again, try to determine if you are spending too much time with the guys every weekend or being self-indulgent, and leaving the wife at home to manage the kids and family single handedly.

Some men's attitude toward their wives seems to say, "I bought you a nice house and a nice car, and I get you everything you want, so I don't feel guilty having a little fun doing what I want to do." This can even be worse with empty nesters because the spouse may have nothing to do except wait on her husband to get home, crash in the recliner, and ask her to get him a beer. I have had several friends whose lives are totally wrapped around golf. Beware, men; you may be asking for problems down the road. Hopefully, you have a wife that copes well with your indulgences.

I am not forgetting there can be role reversal here where the wife, who may also work, may be into sports, biking, or a serious time-consuming exercise regimen, and may be the busy time culprit in the marriage.

I am trying to point out that life should be all about balance and there is no magic formula or exact amount of time married people and their children should all spend together. So much depends on the personalities of the people in the family unit. Couples must be able to talk freely about the distribution of time spent in the Family and Friends circles. Holding frequent conversations with your spouse is essential for open communication and a healthy relationship.

Another factor that affects balance is the children, how many are into sports, how involved are they, and whether their performances and schedules impact the family or affect their behavior. Once again, it is all about balancing the Family circle with Friends and, to a much lesser degree, Self circles. Neither mother nor father should be the only one who always attends their children's games unless there are no alternatives. These are also great opportunities for grandparents to attend as well.

The nicest kids I have met at kid's sports events have two parents present whenever it is possible. It makes a difference. Some parents don't show up at all, and I feel bad for their kids. Neither my father nor mother ever saw me play any sport a single time in my entire life growing up. They didn't ever ask who won when I got home. By now, have you got a pretty good idea of how supportive and balanced your family life is or should be? Does yours need to be adjusted very soon?

I want to discuss an interesting use of the Life Circles by sharing Family and Friends circles. What if two or more couples agree to share the responsibility of their kids in sports or any other events and activities where they all are not only friends but sometimes share meals, playtimes, carpools, etc. to the mutual benefit of both or all parties. Then, you can overlap the two circles. Families that share can save hours each week in this manner and it pleases everyone. The kids and their parents become closer friends, which pleases God and makes them happier because they all have more time available for other things.

I see this with one of my daughters, who is an interior designer and manages a sometimes-frenzied schedule with both her daughters' school and sports activities that otherwise might create an occasional scheduling impossibility. It is great to overlap those two circles whenever it can be done effectively. Sharing must be a two-way street in which you take the load off another family when they need help. Figure 4 shows how sharing provides more free time for both parties. You might also have a different sort of problem if you over share your life with your friends, so try to gauge what you do together and try not to do everything with only one set of friends. It might wear thin over time.

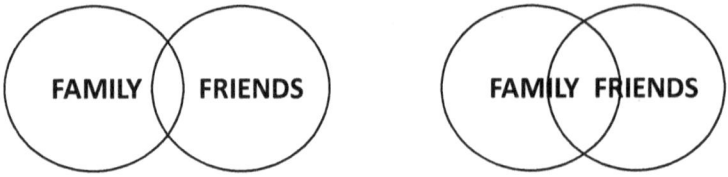

Figure 4. Examples of Different Amounts of Sharing

Until now, I have had little to say about mealtime. I wish to point out a gripe I have. I am astounded when I go out for an evening meal and see heads bowed at the next table and each person or at least two are busy with their cell phones. The first time I saw it happen, I thought they were saying the blessing. My wife had to inform me that they were texting. It is unusual for me to even answer my cell in that situation and certainly off limits if the family is with me.

We always try to say a blessing before we begin to eat, and those around the table are expected to hold conversations, an art that seems lost on some families today. If you have this problem in your family, change it as quickly as you can, e.g., start this evening if you can.

Mealtime affords a wonderful opportunity to tell each other what happened that day and share opinions, current events, and each other's company. Life is so short we shouldn't waste it on complete nonsense like texting. We have even caught two people sitting across from each other not talking but rather texting each other and finally agreeing on what they want to eat. I suppose practice makes perfect. What a great honor it would be to be awarded the Best Texter Award at your school or job. Not!

Thus, one of my objectives of this book is also to point out silly things people do and try to convince them to stop doing them. When you believe God is omnipresent and omniscient, that should be enough to elevate the conversation to a higher plane. Mealtime together is an extremely important daily event lost to some people . . . try hard to get it back in your family if it has slipped away.

It is little things you do that often turn out to be important and add up to convince your family you love and care about them more than anything else in your life except for God.

You can quote me on this: Silent meals are an indication of far deeper negative issues in your relationship. It is not necessarily a cause, but it certainly is a symptom. And my last thought is that kids can be excused if necessary to start homework or whatever is necessary, but husbands and wives should normally clean up after the meal together. It should not be the same person's job every evening.

While I think of it, today's children do not for the most part have enough chores—routine things they are expected to do every day and every week. Make a list of what yours are expected to do daily and/or weekly. It may surprise you that you have a blank entry.

I know several men who still cut their grass and care for their yards while their teenage kids don't lift a finger to help. If you are one of these parents, I urge you to begin now to get your kids involved with this thing called responsibility; it is one of the greatest character builders in the world. They will thank you someday when they are the ones who get better jobs because they have better work ethics. It makes God sad when you don't teach your children a value system. It is never too late to start.

It may shock kids terribly when you tell them the yard needs cutting and clean-up, leaves need raking and bagging, and now is a good time to begin. While they are staring at you, say "right now!" And mean it. I said earlier, it is never too late to begin. You can remind them when everyone pitches in and works together, it can be fun and won't take long at all. When I was a teenager, I cut our grass and my grandmother's grass with a push mover. That means one without a motor on it. Tell your kids you appreciate their helping around the house. You should have brought them up to offer to help do things around the house as well as the yard without being asked. If this happens without a lot of urging on your part, congratulations, you have taught your children an important principle that will stay with them their entire lives. I also notice trash in office buildings and on the sidewalk that was carelessly discarded, and I pause for a second and pick it up and put it in a trash can. Unfortunately, there are a lot of people too lazy or uncaring to do this. If your children see you do this, they will hopefully learn from your examples.

Please save your little circles, because you will want to see how much re-balancing you need to do and hopefully understand the benefits to you and your family for doing so. I would also invite you to pause in reading the book long enough to write a list of things that are going well in your life and another list of things that are problematic. Feel free to add to these lists as you continue to read the book. Ultimately you may want or even need to share these two lists with your spouse.

2

Is Your Job Running Your Life?

NOW WE MUST TURN around and look back at the first circle we drew, the Work circle. Is it so large that it dwarfs the Family and Friends circle? Or is it larger than the two others combined? Does it exceed the 45 hours a week, which is the nominal work and commuting time for most people? A lot of people have a job they are very proud of, or has them convinced they are indispensable, or they are afraid of losing, or they really hate but are going to tough it out, or demands way too much from them, etc.

It is most likely that millions of people just here in the United States don't like their jobs and want to change, but don't feel they can. In fact, some people are too busy or too unsure of themselves to even look for a new job. A book I read recently urged people who feel these things to quit and find something else to do. I can honestly say I have had two jobs like that in my life, quit both eventually, and found my new ones much better and more satisfying than the old ones.

In fact, that last bad job had so much stress it gave me a quadruple bypass. I speak with the authority of one who has been there and done that. I urge you if your job has you really stressed out, go do something else. Your life and your family's life are not worth wrecking your health over a bad job.

What I once thought was the best job I ever had turned out to be the worst job I ever had, and I blame management; they kept piling on more and more work and I kept trying to do it all and I finally got smart, retired, and started doing what I really like doing. I have been happy for 12 years now, and best of all, I am joyful to be alive every day of my life. Even when life's storms come along, I know there will be a rainbow.

I recently read a book whose author asserted this idea: that you are either about to enter a bad time, are in a bad time now, or you are just getting over a bad time. In other words, he believed life here on earth was one catastrophe after another. Poor man! What an incredibly negative way of looking at life. I guess for some people this could be true, which makes to me sad for them.

I believe each day is a glorious event in which I can always find something to be grateful for and appreciate—flowers in full bloom, rain, sunshine, a deer eating one of my shrubs, an early morning mist, snow—nature screams for us to look at God's Glory; it is all around us every day of our lives. The best part, it is completely free, just there for us to appreciate.

I love to watch people walking in a park on a sunny day or shopping and laughing and having fun just being alive, and kids doing the same funny things generation after generation. If you get bored, hang out in Target with a cup of coffee and just watch people for 30 minutes. Most of them are happy, which speaks well for humanity. Take a drive in the country or walk along a river bank and see that no two ripples are ever quite the same. Stare in the water long enough and you may see fish looking back at you or little fresh-water mussels filtering the water. God designed the earth to be self-sustaining and in balance. These examples are what is meant by "take time to smell the roses," and you can be happy in your heart regardless of your situation.

When you find your job has you so stifled and stressed you cannot see God's Glory in everyday life, you need a new job as soon as you can find one. I have done that three or four times in my life. When I felt stale or the job became a drudgery instead of a challenge, I just simply found something else to do to make a living, and each time I found out later I had done the right thing. I must tell you I prayed a lot before I made each change and some inner voice gave me reassurance that I was doing the right thing. I really believe the Holy Spirit is that voice.

Your job should not be the most important thing in your life. First should come your faith, family, and then your friends. If you are single, it should still be the same three.

Let us turn back about 30 or so years and discuss another bad job I had. I had a boss who decided to call me one Saturday evening about 9 o'clock and told me to come in Sunday morning and discuss a proposal and pending new opportunities, so I did. The following weekend, the same thing happened, so being conscientious, I agreed, and for the next couple of months my family lost me most Sunday mornings.

Finally, one day I went to see him and explained that I had a wife and children who share my life and I was finished wrecking my Sundays and missing church. It was never quite the same between the two of us after that. I was no longer his fair-haired protégé.

It wasn't too long before I saw the handwriting on the wall and quit that job of 14 years and went elsewhere. My family life got a lot better and I carved out a new career with a different company that did essentially the same kind of work as the old company, and I was happy for the first time in years.

The biggest blessing and hence accomplishment of all with the new job was that I had time to sit at home and write a textbook, which was published by John Wiley and Sons. That gave me many opportunities that changed my life, opened doors I didn't know existed, and gave me and my family opportunities to travel all over the United States, Canada, and even Europe.

My book had filled a niche. Several universities added it to their curriculum. People were calling me from all over the country. It gave me opportunities to teach and lecture at the university level, attend lots of seminars, and write more than 30 technical papers for presentation at major conferences. I felt I had arrived where I always wanted to be, and I thanked God for my good fortune.

None of these things would have happened if I hadn't changed the path I was on, and God was no doubt guiding me along the way. I must admit I had a great family support system and friends whom I respected and loved. I was able to take my wife and youngest child to many of these places. This was also a time in my life when I had prayed very hard that my decision to change jobs was the right thing to do. You may ask if I got an answer to that prayer? I know that I did. But I must admit, it came on God's time line, not mine. I realized how fortunate I was years later.

Sometimes you think God doesn't hear you, but it is not the right time for his reply, so sometimes you must be very patient. He also passes judgment on your prayers and just maybe on occasion you ask for something that God believes you do not need and he turns you down. Analyze what you pray for and determine if you are asking too much and being selfish.

Therefore, my conclusion is that a well-timed departure is sometimes the best thing you can do with your life and that of your family. I urge you to pray about such decisions because we tend to be afraid, sometimes, to venture into the unknown. View changing jobs as a great adventure, and you must be totally committed that you are going to make the best of the situation. I found it to be invigorating and challenging, and you get to make new friends and acquaintances and get new projects to work on. Decide you are going to learn new things wherever you go.

There is a small warning that comes with this advice: We should not make snap decisions about our jobs. I have known a couple of people who were so on the edge of being burned out that one simply walked out of work one day and didn't come back and the other at least wrote a letter of resignation before he went and found a box and cleaned out his desk and then left. This is called burning bridges and hurts your reputation when looking for jobs in the future, so do some planning and looking for that new job before you leave the current one and give a reasonable notice (usually two weeks).

Once you are committed to change, it is usually best if you leave, even if the current employer offers you more money to stay, because you will seldom be viewed quite the same as you were before you tried to quit and decided to stay on. There are exceptions to this, but you should assess the reasons you were willing to quit in the first place and go from there.

In looking to go elsewhere, you would be wise to make a list of likes and dislikes about both places and it will help you judge the advantages of the new opportunity. If you are married, talk it over with your spouse and both of you pray about it. Don't quit if the new job is only marginally better than the old one; look some more before you move.

You need to improve your job satisfaction, your compensation, your growth potential, and sometimes your commute when you change jobs. It has to feel right, so be very quiet and listen to your inner voice. Then talk it over with your spouse. Be sure to get the facts on their benefits, including medical insurance, because that is one area that is totally out of control in many small businesses or if you are buying an individual or single-family policy outside of a group plan. All the politicians in Washington talk a lot about it, but none of them really appreciates how bad it is, because they get it as a free perk for being an elected official.

I also want you to be prepared to talk to your spouse after you complete reading this book and tell her (or possibly him) that you realize there are things you are doing that you need to change and that you love her (or him), what those things are, and when the changes are going to happen. As you do this, solicit feedback and pay close attention to those feelings and inputs to help reinforce your decisions for changing jobs. Your spouse is your best friend, whether you know or think it sometimes. And after a few years of marriage, your spouse will know you better than anyone else in your life, including your parents.

No long-term relationship such as a marriage is completely free of disagreements and conflicts. I mostly tried to hide those times when I was really put out at my wife over something to do with the children or some decision that seemed important at the time. But as it turned out, most of our big disagreements were about my work, and once I told her I had found a new job and was ready to quit the old one, she would be happy to reinforce my decision. She never doubted me personally. That is a very great compliment you can pay your mate. I never gave her opportunity to doubt me or my motives because I believed in the sacredness of our vows and she did too.

When you began this chapter and if you are someone who feels burned out, unfulfilled, or that something big is lacking in your work or the environment, write it down and begin to analyze it. Write down all your negatives and then write all the positives.

Can some or even most of your negatives about your current job be corrected if given enough time? If the answer is no, start the job search.

For example, in my mid-career, I was required to travel a lot and at times for a few months at a time, requiring that I rent a house in El Paso, Texas. Another time, we lived for three months in a Holiday Inn in Baltimore. The staff got to know us on a first name basis. That would have driven some wives crazy, but my wife took it all in stride and our 5-year-old daughter thought it was a big adventure. They made her an honorary lifeguard at the pool and she helped clean up the pool and the area around it. We ate out every meal for 3 months. The job was great, and we managed very nicely.

I am telling you this story to remind you that sometimes a long TDY job is not the end of the world; it is how you manage it and go with the flow and not get angry at each other. We treated it like a big adventure and did a lot of sightseeing in Washington and around Maryland and Northern Virginia on weekends and ate a lot of great seafood dinners. I am urging you to make the best of whatever situation you find yourselves in. However, when you cannot find enough good things about the job to offset the bad things, go find a different job. Someone gives you lemons, make a lemon pie.

Now let's take the case where you are mildly unhappy or dissatisfied with your job. If you happen to live in a large urban area where commuting time is your most severe problem and you are spending a couple of hours each day at 20 miles an hour on a freeway, here is an idea. You need to propose to the company higher-ups that you love the company and love your work, but your commute is starting to affect your health and your family life. You miss too many of your kid's key events and whatever else you can discuss with them and ask to become a work-at-home employee for two or more days a week.

You may become a hero in the company if you can sell the idea. They may balk, but they will also recognize that you are most likely not the only employee with a problem. It's worth a try. Sometimes, management just needs a prod to begin thinking about their options. No company wants to have their employees have to put up with working conditions that affect their performance or attitude.

If you are the boss of a business and are reading this, poll your employees to see if flex hours would give them a better work plan. Get their participation in offering suggestions that can improve working conditions. Employees always have definite opinions but are usually reluctant to voice them unless asked.

If you are entering the job market for the first time, you need to shop for the most convenient location or be willing to move, if necessary, to have a minimum commute. Examine the long-term plans the company has for its employees and ask a lot of questions of the human resources (HR) person who handles your application and schedules your interviews. HR may tell you things that could impact your accepting or rejecting the job. For example, HR might say the company is planning to move from this location to another which is miles closer or farther away early next year, so you might want to consider that in your decision. Workplace relocation always results in all sorts of impacts—emotional attachments, losing friends, financial impacts (+ and -), trying to make new friends, learning new surroundings, etc. If you have to move, try to look at it as a big adventure. Look for the positives and try to minimize the negatives.

When interviewing, HR is also the right place to ask about benefits, not the technical people and managers for whom you may eventually work. Talk about your short- and long-term goals with the latter group and show a strong interest in what the company does even if you aren't very interested in that position. Every chance you get to be interviewed gives you more experience, reduces your anxiety, makes it easier to tell people about yourself and your skills, education, and areas of expertise.

Put whatever relevant experience you have into a thoroughly proofread resume of no more than one page if you are experience-limited (as would be the case if you are applying for an entry level position) and two pages if you have enough for at least another half page. Don't ramble but keep statements brief except for your goal statement, which should be tailored to the job being advertised.

A well-written resume may not ensure you get the job, but a bad one with misspelled words could keep you from getting a job you really want. I hope you choose your opportunities well.

Another piece of advice is that it is better to be over-dressed (shirt and tie) than to be under-dressed for a job interview, and even though you emailed or mailed in your resume, have a couple of copies with you in case the interviewer misplaces his or hers. Sometimes people seek help writing their resume. If you have done this, make absolutely certain that they have not overstated your experience and that you are thoroughly familiar with its contents including dates, previous employers, etc. Do not use personal references unless you first ask them for their support.

Before an interview, always turn off your cell phone; because even if it vibrates in your pocket, it will distract you. Better yet, leave it in the car.

After shaking hands with the interviewer, say something to relax you both, something complimentary if possible like, "getting here was quite easy for me," or "the day has turned out to be very nice outside," or "this is a very nice facility," or "I was very excited when I saw this job advertised on your job site. It is what I have been looking for." These are called "ice breakers."

As mentioned earlier, if you are only mildly interested in the first response you get job hunting, accept the interview and do as well with it as you can, show interest, and smile a good bit, because each interview opportunity builds your self-confidence and makes you less nervous. Thank the interviewer for his or her time.

Another thought is that security clearances are essential in today's government and many government contractor positions.

Therefore, a company willing to go through that process with you (which costs them money) has provided you a ticket from now on when shopping in the high-tech job market. It is another reason never to be arrested for anything, because it could affect your getting a clearance. Once you have a clearance, negotiate each job you take to continue it, so it will not be dropped, if at all possible.

A final word of warning is that no matter how strong you think your marriage is, and no matter how you like a new job that is half a continent or more away from where you live now, you had better be prepared to reverse it if you find you have to. Early in my working career, I moved our family from New Jersey to Boulder, Colorado in the mid-1960s to take a new job and hopefully get my first wife out of serious post-partum depression, all of which were bad choices. It was a colossal mistake, and even though we only lived there a year and then moved back to New Jersey and I got my old job back, it marked the beginning of the end of that marriage.

So the lesson in this case is serious relocations cause lots of pressure on a marriage, your Friends circle practically disappears, your kids don't know anybody in their school, your wife doesn't know a soul, you can't find a church you like, you don't know where to shop, you can't find a doctor or dentist you like, your personal infrastructure is destroyed and it destroys the good things in life you had before.

I didn't know better in those days and you have probably heard "ignorance is no excuse;" well, it is all I can blame it on. I made a dumb mistake. So, bear in mind that it certainly proved to me my job is not the most important thing in my life. Don't let your life rotate around your job. Instead, anchor your life in your family, friends, and spiritual life. "It takes a village to raise a child" is an old African proverb and seems appropriate, in this case, to make a family whole and happy. Although we returned to my wife's roots, the damage was done. Our marriage began to deteriorate—first like a little trickle of a leak, then a little stream of discontent, which enlarged its own hole until it was a river and there was no stopping it until the day she just walked out the door and didn't come back.

I also discuss jobs and bosses I have had in other chapters as well, so by the time you finish this book you should have a pretty good idea how good your job is, or if you need to consider changing it to improve your marriage and your life. A little food for thought is perhaps it is worth having at least one really bad job in your life so you can appreciate a good one when you land it. If you always give the company you work for a fair day's work, you should never feel guilty when it is time to leave them for something better. You will make new friends and find new challenges, all of which keeps you sharp and interested in doing the best you can.

3

I Have A Lot To Say
To Young People

YOUNG PEOPLE WHO HAVE yet to enter their career path can either leave off the Work circle or may morph the Work circle into the Military or College obligated time, which could easily take more than 45 hours a week if they are carrying a full load. Either path is like a career, and remember, these are temporary decision circles. I would love to see their circles. A typical college student's circles tend to be weighted toward Friends and Self with Family third. This is often driven by their dislocation from their family.

A military person today is typically one who commits his or her life for a defined period to serve their country and when the enlistment is up, must decide to either stay or get out. Their circles are dominated by the very large Military circle that takes over the Work circle and leaves small Family, Friends, and Self circles. Both the military person and the college student share similar circles.

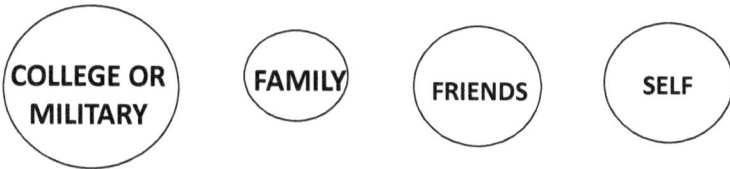

Figure 5. Examples of College and Military Circles

The important thing with college students is to remind them from time to time that they are still part of the family (said with a chuckle) and you love them and are very pleased they are working hard to get an education and you are still providing them with many essentials. Give them much looser reins than when they were in high school, especially if they still live at home.

It is still easy to fool ourselves that they will still take parental advice, but probably will to a degree if you continue to support them while in college. You must stop giving them advice on most things unless they ask for it. Do not use the old very offensive cliché "As long as you are under my roof you'll do what I say." I heard that one quite often. That will just about always blow up in your face and doesn't work well at all. Rejoice if they still really like coming home, and not just to do laundry. Just try not to either hover over or over-control them, because it won't work, and they will only resent it. They are trying very hard to grow up fast and need to be able to count on their patents to be the stable force in their lives and not an interference factor.

Young people who maintain good relationships with their families are indeed lucky, because family is the best support system there is, and it never goes away.

From the time I was 16 years old, I was a radio announcer and DJ and had a lot of fun for three years and then the radio station built a TV station and my whole life changed . . . I went into a new career and learned literally every job at the TV station—staff announcer, did the 10 PM news for 30 minutes by myself, edited all the film every day, sometimes ran a talk show, MC'd a Saturday dance party, helped out on an afternoon kids show, built sets for local shows, ran the control room most nights a week, and did camera work occasionally . . . eight or more jobs, which took 80 to 100 hours every week, and I was trying to go to college while working that much.

I stuck it out for two years but found I couldn't keep it up, and the things that suffered the most were my college, then family, friends, personal time, and eventually my health. I didn't even have time to think about the downward spiral I was on. Meanwhile, I was learning a lot about TV production, engineering, film, taking pictures, running a TV station, how to do interviews, how to ad-lib in any situation, etc. I thought all the while that this would be my life-long career. How did it all turn out?

I was also in the National Guard as a sergeant, so I volunteered to go on active duty to radar school at Ft. Monmouth, NJ, and walked away from the first job that I loved because I needed to get my health back and to have some breathing room away from my family and living at home, which had become extremely stifling. Radar school was 8 hours a day for 9 months and a terrific way to get away from everything in my past life and start over with a fresh perspective on everything. I loved it and I loved being in the Army. It was a huge departure from everything in my past.

I loved it so much I stayed in New Jersey after the Army duty ended and got a job working in New York City down on Church Street in lower Manhattan, very close to where the World Trade Center once stood. At this point, my life circles went to near normal for the first time in my life and I felt ready to settle down.

I got married and we saved our money and in two years we bought our first house. A year or so later, a job opened in New Jersey, so I no longer had to commute into the Big Apple. By that time, the gloss had worn off my idea of working in New York City. I went back to college at Rutgers for the next 6 years at night, and every Monday and Thursday night that I had classes, I ate a hamburger, fries, and Coke at McDonalds and got change back from my dollar for the first few years. My, how times have changed!

Each of you who reads this may find my life jumps around a bit, and I can assure you it did just that. I had to do some things the hard way to get through them, but it paid off in the long run.

Hopefully, most of you who read this will go straight through college and get your degree in four years and then enter the work force, or perhaps some will continue for a Master's, which today is a very good idea and often puts you higher up in the companies for which you work.

I do not recommend doing what I did, because interrupting a degree is never a good idea and many times you end up never going back or going to night school for a much longer time than if you just stuck it out right after high school.

This brings up another piece of advice: when you are in college, try not to work at a job more than 15 or at most 20 hours a week, and less if you can afford to, because your grades are extremely important and will follow you for the next 20 or so years whenever you apply for a new job. A higher GPA means higher pay when entering the job force in a lot of companies. College should be more than just getting any old degree; it should prepare you for something you like doing. Try not to have it force you into doing something that in a short while after graduation turns out to be mediocre.

Let's talk a bit more about the military. If you are graduating from high school and have no idea what field you want to go into and you don't feel you are ready to start college or simply can't afford it, the military offers you very good alternatives.

Once you get through basic training, all the Services offer you opportunities to learn a skilled trade. But you must have that high school diploma because they pretty much use that to screen out under-achievers. In other words, all the Services want highly skilled people on whom they can depend.

In a few years in the military, if you find you don't want to make it your long-term career, there are many civilian jobs you can find when you get out that require the skills you received from your military training. For example, they train people to be air traffic controllers, radar operators or repairmen, all kinds of computer-based skills including cyber security and network management, IT, meteorology, jet engine repair, guided missile systems, and vehicle maintenance to name a few. So, there are a rich number of specialties to select from and you are paid to learn them, which is quite the opposite from college. I chose radar school, which set me up for an excellent job when I got out of the Army.

Some service jobs will also allow or even send you to college while you are in the military, depending on your performance and the skills required for the job. So, all in all, it may be an attractive alternative to going to college right after high school. By the way, it pays a lot better than when I was in the service.

Let's turn our attention back to college. If you decide on college, the two biggest decisions you need to make are selecting your major and deciding what college you want to attend, and they are sort of co-dependent as I will explain. There is a lot of information on the Internet to help you, in fact, so much that you can easily be overwhelmed by what some universities do to sell you on their being the place you need to be.

It certainly is nice if you already know where you are going after high school, but often you just aren't sure. So, the first consideration depends on your major and your general aptitude. What talents did God give you? Hopefully you have some idea. They are typically the courses you enjoyed and breezed through and not the ones that gave you anxiety. If you do well in science and mathematics in high school, you would likely be a suitable candidate for engineering or something scientific and you would be putting your inherent talents to appropriate use.

Then, the logical next step is to narrow the field and perhaps look only at science and engineering schools. There are lots of them nowadays. That is what I meant by co-dependent. You would not go to a liberal arts college for engineering, any more than a language major would pick an engineering school.

Thus, base your selection on the general field you are interested in and focus on getting into the school that meets your other criteria such as location, cost, reputation, potential for part-time work, etc. State universities are usually the least expensive with many sources of scholarship money, and many of them specialize to some extent. Incidentally, scholarships usually require you to keep your grades up, so that is a good forcing function.

Using a simple method like this helps you to narrow your choices of schools to no more than ten candidates, with four or five being much better, which is a manageable number. The more selective you become early, the better, because so many young people enter college and a year or two later change their major, and sometimes for a third time, and what happens is they have accrued some course credits that don't apply to their major and they turn a four-year degree program into five years and add about 20 percent to the cost of their education.

If you decide on a big state university, be prepared to cope with the sheer size of most of these campuses and make sure you like riding a bicycle to class in rain, snow, and sweltering heat. Some people elect to start at a junior college or private university, which are generally much smaller and have a lot to offer because you won't feel as lost from the start.

My oldest daughter went to a small state university that had an enrollment of maybe 2500 at that time, which is small by today's standards, so that size didn't bother her. Whereas, our youngest daughter went to a private Christian university in Nashville and found it to be a truly great experience. She married a great guy who was also a student there. Smaller schools are less frustrating to the student and generally offer a great learning experience and less stressful social environment. Pick the school that feels right for you.

The number and variety of schools has never been as great as it is today, and there are a funds available from many sources for students with good grades and high ACT scores. All I can say is good luck and apply yourself, and pray you made the right choice. Enjoy yourself as much as possible because it can be a cruel world out there if you aren't prepared to meet it head on. A college degree helps but isn't the end-all panacea that ensures you a good life from now on. You will still have hurdles and difficulties sometimes, so remember the things I mentioned in Chapter 2. You may work at several jobs before you feel that you finally found the one you have always wanted, so do not be afraid to change jobs, especially when you are young. Even after you feel settled into a job you like, it will probably not be the one you stay with for your entire life. In fact, statistics say you are likely to change jobs several times during your career.

Just remember, it is more than the money they pay you that will give you job satisfaction. Every job includes intangibles you discover only after you work there a while that make it worthwhile or not, and many of your discoveries concern the people you work with. They can make it for you or break it. Some lines of work, especially creative jobs, can sometimes milk you for your good ideas, and you may find your work being presented in the conference room to management by your boss as his or her ideas. It is hard to protect yourself in those organizations. You put up with it or you quit; there are not many choices in between.

So, when starting a new job before you get to know who you can trust and who you cannot, lock up your stuff or take it home with you in a briefcase or thumb drive every night, especially if it has any connections to your creative, artistic, or literary talents. Make sure you protect your ideas and don't leave them lying around where others can see and possibly steal your work. It happens more often than you can imagine.

Upon leaving one large company some years ago, I was challenged to surrender all my intellectual property, and I broke out laughing and had trouble stopping. I was finally able to say I brought more intellectual property to this company than I ever derived from being here. Companies do have certain rights to intellectual property developed while you are working for them and normally ask you to sign a paper when you are hired that you will forfeit such property when leaving the company. This is part of the protection companies afford themselves, so you cannot run off with their great ideas, even though they may be your original ideas.

I would like to add that some of the best ideas for new products and product improvements come from new employees because they have fresh ideas and are not locked into the corporate culture that sometimes believes "We have always done it this way at Company ABC and we'll keep doing it that way as long as I am President."

Ford Motor Company is a notable example of this way of thinking while Henry Ford Senior was still around. He would walk through the plant and experimental labs and if he found a six-cylinder engine being developed, he would get a sledge hammer, smash it to bits, and no doubt fire everyone who had worked on it. It had better be a V8. He hated sixes, probably because his biggest competitor was Chevrolet, and everything they had in that era was sixes.

Despite some of his quirky ideas, Henry was also an innovative genius. The wooden crates from certain Ford suppliers had to be made to rigorous specifications because when the parts were removed, the crates were carefully taken apart and the nails removed, and they became the floor boards of his famous Model Ts. He also started Kingsford Charcoal to use up leftover charcoal from his steel-making operation. He was truly one of America's great entrepreneurs. None of us will likely become another Henry Ford, but he is a very interesting study because he didn't ever waste things. If he were alive today and given the challenge, he could probably figure out what to do with all the plastic sacks and wrappings we throw away every day that are polluting our planet.

When you are starting your first job, set your goals high and don't settle for a job you can do with your eyes closed; go for the ones with a challenge, work hard and get used to doing your share and then a little bit more. That sort of work ethic is part of what made America in the 1900s a great nation that out-produced every other country in the world. We have lost some of that zeal somewhere along the way, so hopefully the current generation entering the job market will bring some of that spirit back.

Remember also that you do not have to be a college graduate to make a success of your life and find a meaningful job. There are thousands of skilled technical jobs in all sorts of industries and service organizations, and many will send you to school for the necessary training and certifications. Enjoy the variability and challenge of one of the popular new careers and try not to just settle for mediocre or unchallenging work.

The world is your oyster and you just need to figure out how to pop the shell open.

It is now time to raise the intensity of the discussions about our Life Circles, so follow me to Chapter 4.

4

More Information on
Your Life Circles

WHEN I BEGAN THIS book, I found it more difficult to write than technical documents because it is about life forces and emotional and spiritual things and not about technical things. Throughout my career I have done engineering and scientific things and worked on hardware and software systems and have written about those topics a great deal. I have also taught over 60 seminars and short courses on a variety of technical and management subjects in which largely deterministic conclusions can be had. Mathematics is consistent and gives the same answer every time you make the same calculation, but things of the heart and human relationships, and how and why they function the way they do and sometimes even fail to function, can be very challenging to analyze and address.

This points to the conclusion that exact answers about how to run your life effectively and efficiently simply do not exist, but rather we take examples that worked for others and try to apply them to our lives, even though they may not be a perfect fit. Answers based on human responses and emotions will vary all over. Life Circles help because the size of the circles we generate for ourselves are telling and convincing that we must change some of the bad habits and imbalances we find. Until you draw these circles you don't appreciate their relative importance to you and your family's well-being.

Many years ago, I studied Venn diagrams and was intrigued by the simple, yet elegant ways they could show relationships and convey ideas, so I use some of these techniques to explain my thoughts and reasoning where it adds to understanding. Circles have no loose ends or corners where things can hide. Everything you place in a circle belongs to a common set of things. Therefore, if I make a circle called Family it automatically represents my family. In my notation, the larger I make the circle the more emphasis I place on the number of hours spent relative to a standard week which has 168 hours, about a third of which is spent in the bedroom and bathroom. I already explained how this works in Chapter 1 but decided to wait until now to explain what happens when you overlay any two of your circles as shown in Figure 6.

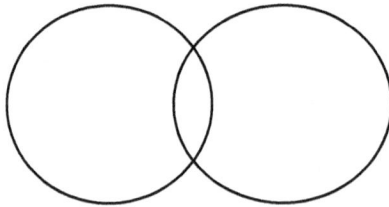

Figure 6. More About Sharing Life Circles

When two circles overlap, it shows several things: they share certain common things such as the same people or characteristics. In this case, it is typically people, such as some of your family and also very often some of your close friends. The degree of overlap can show relative amounts of coupling. If the two circles do not touch, then your family does not know or associate with your friends. This case would be if your golfing buddies never met your wife and their wives never met each other. This could be a deliberate isolation so that whatever happens on your golf trips "stays in Vegas." The same rule in Venn diagrams can be shown by putting an X in the overlap zone. It disassociates the two groups. In any case, it is no doubt healthier if Family and Friend circles have some overlap. The wives might even want to get together and play golf themselves or tennis or cards, whatever, or all go to a day spa or eat lunch together. Men, the message is what's good for the gander is good for the goose and vice versa. Bear that in mind. You will have noticed I said it backward because it is usually the gander's lead that takes away available family time, and not the goose's, although the roles can certainly be reversed.

Remember to size the circles in proportion to their number of hours per week they contain, and earlier I cautioned you when your Friends circle is larger than your Family circle week after week, you could be headed for a significant problem in the future if it persists. Now, if it happens only occasionally, it is probably okay, but even then, it should be accompanied by doing something extra nice for your spouse.

What I am trying to teach you throughout this book is balance. Do things to balance your circle with her circle or circles. For every trip or weekend day you go off with the guys, she is most likely going to spend that time looking after and doing things for the kids that you don't see because you are gone. I think it is called being a soccer mom. Remember not to try to buy her off with flowers or gifts. She will become immediately suspicious if you do, but taking her to dinner will probably be okay, especially if you say it's a reward for being so sweet and considerate.

My earlier caution was that if your Friends circle is larger than your Family circle consistently, you are out of balance and living your life with a growing likelihood that it may not hold together or at least things may get a little rough. What are other consequences besides a divorce in your future? Let's examine a few. When you devote too much attention to your fun and games, your children sense it and know they aren't as important to you as your golf or whatever it is, so they begin to resent that part of you. They see their mother trying to compensate and they try to love her more intensely because they sense her sadness and it makes cracks in the bonds and oneness you once had with everyone in your immediate family.

I saw it in my family as a child, not from my father's Friends circle, but because he worked too much on his own things when he was at home. He was extremely self-indulgent. If I asked him how to spell a word he'd fuss because I interrupted whatever he was doing. So I learned not to bother him and I turned to my mother who was quite patient. Later in my life, I realized I didn't have much real affection for my father because he never showed his love outwardly and never simply said, "I love you." Not until he was in his mid-seventies and I was putting in a French drain in his yard did he tell he loved me, and I wept and asked him why it took all those years to tell me, and he said he thought I knew he did, and I said, "you have to tell someone you love them, or they are never going to be sure if you never say it!"

To their credit, both my parents encouraged me in almost every endeavor I attempted growing up. When I was young, my father would let me do things he knew were not necessarily correct, so I would learn for myself what works and what doesn't. He would sometimes give me a broken clock or an old radio that didn't work and I would take them apart and spend hours learning all the parts and sometimes I got them working again. The point I want to make is this: God wants us to learn as much as we can to think for ourselves, and to have good judgment. Moreover, at the same time, He expects us to respect him as our Father and give him credit for giving us the talents and abilities that let us cope with the intricacies of life here on earth in preparation for life everlasting. The balance lies in not becoming haughty and egotistical, but in having the good sense to thank God for our abilities and good works.

The parallel between our heavenly Father and our natural father is so obvious, but I still must talk about it a little more. When I got in trouble a few times in my teens, who did I turn to? My father, and he was solid as a rock when those times came, and he was very understanding and forgiving, and he helped me get past them and get on with my life. At the same time, I was praying to God the Father for forgiveness, love, and understanding. I wasn't sure at that time in my life that God heard my prayers. Now I know he did, but I think he was waiting to see how I coped. We are on his timetable, not ours.

It was later when I started college that neither parent had the sense to give me room to begin setting my own agenda and living my own life. They actually regressed and wanted to apply more control, which didn't work well at all. In retrospect, if I could have afforded it, which I couldn't, I should have moved out of their house and either lived in the dorm or an apartment. But I didn't have that option and I have told you the rest of that story elsewhere in the book. When you become an adult, you should turn to God first when you have problems, and maybe secondarily to your parents, depending on the circumstances. As long as you have family, there is always some need to seek their approval and support with the big decisions in your life, or when you have problems that you cannot solve by yourself.

So what lessons did I learn growing up from these experiences? Lots of things, I guess, but most certainly to tell your children you love them frequently, so they never doubt it. Children have perceptions about interpersonal relationships that are amazingly accurate, mostly because they sense things without consciously thinking about them and their moods will change, and they cannot explain their feelings, but they are very real and mostly very honest because they do not yet know how to lie about them. They can just sense things are amiss. Therefore, my advice is do not alienate your children with your own self-indulgences either with or without your friends in the loop. Be conscious of the attention you give your children, love them, and tell them you do every chance you get. You will never regret telling them every day. I do it a lot.

So many marriages today are second or sometimes third-time events that the children need special attention and lots of behavioral consistency so that they can better understand you. In a mixed setting, your natural children will tend to come to you for favors and not their new step-parent, so you must continuously explain to them calmly from the beginning that their new combined parents love and accept them, and all decisions are going to be made as impartially as possible because you both want to be completely fair to all the members of the combined family.

Make it a point to never yell at any of the children in these situations. Just stay calm and loving and be a peacemaker, not the dictator. I have seen it work extremely well, and other times, not so good. One parent cannot show partiality to his or her own child in decision-making. That never works. If a kid from one side keeps trying to blame a child from the other side for everything that goes wrong, the parents will have a real challenge getting things to work. Fortunately, these things tend to work out better when the kids feel they are all receiving the same judgment and treatment; once again it is a matter of balance.

If visitation isn't well balanced by the court system, it can also cause a significant problem, so you may on occasion have to go back to court to get things better balanced and explain that the visitation arrangement is hurting the children's relationships with each other or one of the parents.

Again, it is all about balance. I believe these things because my first marriage ended after 12 years and my second was more successful than the first and we survived the occasional discontent between my children and her children. All of that is now well in the past, but it teaches you how to cope with a mix of children from both parents. And it does help if you pray about it frequently while it is sorting itself out.

In the beginning of a combined marriage in which children from both sides are going to live together, the Family circle may grow almost disproportionally large and both parents may find their Friends circle shrinks appreciably and the Self circle disappears almost completely for the time being. This is expected, because suddenly the parents are generally overwhelmed and must be very careful to make some private time for the two of them or their marriage can unravel badly.

The kids of a combined marriage must understand that Mom and Dad must have some time to themselves. When they are old enough kids to babysit or have a sitter, the new parents need a date night once a week or so to leave the kids home and go out for a simple dinner, a movie, or whatever they want to do without worrying about the kids. This is a must and should continue for a long time. My wife and I kept date night going every week for many years even after all the kids were gone.

What really helped us through the rough times was that when we met, we had both had several years of bad first marriages that we had tried to salvage until we realized there wasn't anything left to save. We had both tried and failed, so our expectations were realistic, and we truly were in love with each other and realized what we had was very special, not just average, and by then we were mature individuals, both in our early to mid-30s.

We came from the same town, have many common friends, liked the same things and never got bored with each other. It didn't take much to please either of us, and we were both broke as Job's turkey when we got married. In fact, she had $300 and I was in debt to my eyebrows, so we started out in a deep hole. I was spending every penny I made on child support and maintaining two households. We wrote poetry to each other, we wrote beautiful letters to each other, and we basically adored each other. We never yelled at each other about anything and seldom argued and then only when it was about the kids and never about our relationship.

We were both in love and stayed that way our entire lives together. Carolyn died in 2016 after a long illness and it was the saddest day of my life. She was one of the most giving people I have ever known and the most spiritual. When we met, I had fallen from grace and was blaming God for my misfortune and disintegrated first marriage, and she led me back from the edge of spiritual despair and supported my decision to be baptized as an adult, and I came out of the water a different person. It truly was a life-changing thing for me, because it washed away my past sins and failings and gave me a fresh start in my life, which I very badly needed.

I heartily recommend it for someone who was sprinkled as an infant, which I was. My faith came back like it was when I was young, and I began to see things from a different perspective. It allowed me to appreciate God's glory and grace again and it became the spiritual glue that kept our marriage flourishing. It wasn't long after that event that Carolyn announced she was pregnant, and we were both on top of the world and we knew our baby was a special gift from God. It turns out, I have been an extremely lucky person. The baby was definitely unplanned, and I had to borrow money from the bank to get them both out of the hospital, and Carolyn's father had to call the bank president before we could get the loan for $750. I told you we were poor, but rich in so many other ways. I can laugh about it now, but it wasn't too funny at the time.

It took us a long time to get well financially and what helped was I finally agreed to give my ex-wife the house in New Jersey if she and her new husband would take over the deed and mortgage.

We began to very slowly climb out of debt. We shopped at every bargain store in town. My daughters thought IRREG was a brand name.

By this time our Life Circles were pretty balanced but we still had no reserves at all, so I went to a local university and pitched a week-long course on one of my favorite technical subjects and they bought the idea and advertised the course. We had 25 people sign up for $400 each and I took a week of vacation from my regular job, gave the course, and we split the money 50/50, so I made $4000 after we paid for the room at the Civic Center where the class was held.

In a few months, I went to the University of Alabama and signed up as an adjunct professor to do two courses a year and then sometimes three or four a year and the extra money kept coming in, so soon we got better financially. When we finally paid off the last debt, we agreed never to buy anything we couldn't afford or on monthly payments. It is actually a pretty good plan, so I pay cash for everything I buy, and when I use credit cards, I pay the entire bill—usually the day it arrives. We haven't had any debt in 30 years, including for the house.

In the beginning of our marriage, we were barely making it financially, so desperation became the mother of invention and I took the five different courses I developed on the road and taught them all over the country at government facilities and hotels, wherever people wanted me to teach. The purpose of my telling you this story is that when you find yourself in a difficult situation, you must do something proactive about it to make it better. Some people take the easy way out and declare bankruptcy, while others work extra fixing it. It is much better to work it off. God helped me out, too, because nothing bad ever happened to me on any of these sessions.

Want a laugh? I was teaching at Gunter Air Force Base in Montgomery and the lights went out; the room was completely dark with no windows or emergency lights and no one had cell phones in those days. I just went on with my talk until the lights came back on and I never missed a beat. Everyone applauded. That was how well I knew my material. I could do that because I loved what I was doing and it was fun; God gave me that talent and I wasn't going to waste it. Our family reaped the benefits. Most of you are probably familiar with the parable of the talents. The lesson there is if you are given talents, use them wisely and it pleases God, but if you do not use but hide your talent, it displeases God greatly (Matt 25:14–30 and Luke 19:11–27). You should not hide your talents nor should you brag about them, but rather you should use them for God's glory and be grateful you received them. If they help you become successful in life, repay those gifts by being more benevolent and sharing.

If any of my story resonates with you, and you sometimes find your marriage, work, or faith is weaker than you know it should be, or you don't feel right about things, or you think you are wasting your talents, I urge you to speak to your religious leader and seek help and support. This is also when you need to find a quiet spot to pray. It will help, so open your heart and soul to God and ask for His help. Are your Life Circles balanced or a little off?

In addition, your spouse may be holding back, not wanting to upset you by talking to you about it, but sensing something is wrong. We tend to show it in our faces and even our body language when things aren't going well or we are feeling down. Get it out in the open and discuss it, and 90 percent of the time, it will start getting better right away. Keeping things that bother you inside eats away at your spirit and reduces your ability to love the things you treasure—your work, your family, your friends, and God. You must break down these barriers that you, for the most part, have erected to protect yourself, because they never work. Isolation never works. Holding things inside is self-destructive. Ask your family, minister, or good friends to help you, and pray and talk to God about it. You really need others who are willing to listen and help you.

Sometimes when you are feeling down about your life and your marriage, you should go back and flip through your wedding pictures and revisit how you both looked and how you felt on that day and for the first months after you were married. I did that a few years ago and it was cathartic. You and she are still those same two people who had their entire future in front of them. Take about three deep breaths and let them out slowly each time and remember this is your life, your adventure, your love, how lucky you are to have married whom you did, and what a great life you have. Sure, you have a few problems, but you can both overcome them if you resolve to do it starting now.

Sit down with your wife and go back through the album again and tell her how much you love her, how beautiful she is, and how much she means to you, then resolve to work on your biggest problem first and fix it. When that one is done, fix the next one, and then the next. Life throws us all curve balls from time to time and you must be willing to work through them. Don't be willing to throw in the towel too soon. Most family problems have a sensible solution, but you may find it takes work to fix them. Be willing to try. It beats the alternative. Be quick to say you are sorry when you and your spouse have a disagreement.

Our world today is so full of negative thinking, negative news, and people's hatred of other people simply because they live in other counties, perhaps speak a different language, and have different political views. It affects our attitudes and behaviors, it makes us quicker to anger, less tolerant of other opinions, and in general, unhappier than we should be. This nation has never been so polarized as it is today. If children are exposed to much of this infighting, it can give them prejudices against certain types and groups of people. There are more people shooting other people than ever before in our history.

For America, did it begin for us in the Cold War Era when we were supposed to hate entire nations because they didn't agree with our politics? Politics in general is a corrupt way of reaching decisions that should be good for all the people. It is has become much more about trading favors than about doing what is right.

Have we forgotten this country is made up of people from all over the world, the greatest melting pot of different cultures ever assembled on earth? Have we forgotten to take a more global view of this world and realize God made all people and to him we are all beautiful in our own ways and with our own characteristics? God loves us all and made us each a little different. I am sure God gets very disgusted with how we treat each other. He likely reflects on how he gave us ten easy to understand rules to live by and we can't even get those right.

No two of us are quite the same, each an individual, each with the same basic feelings, emotions, awareness, and needs. We need to thank God for how incredibly fortunate and blessed we are to live in America with such countless opportunities for a good life. We must stop fighting among ourselves when so many in this world struggle with finding clean water and something to eat every day. It should make us grateful and more willing to love each other, not hate one another.

I believe one resolution today's parents should make is to teach their children to be kind to everyone. I know they will find it is not a nice world out there sometimes. They will get their feelings hurt sometimes being nice to someone who doesn't know how to respond to kindness. If I had to think of one single attribute a godly person has, it is kindness. Love and kindness go together. If you love someone deeply, you should never want to be mean or hurt them. Bring up your children to be kind in every situation.

5

Starting Out in a Career and Finding a Mate

It seemed to me that there are more unmarried singles than ever before, so I decided to consult some authoritative sources for confirmation. I was correct and found several more surprises in the process; things are worse than I thought. It turns out that US Census data compiled over the last hundred years show that men and women are waiting longer to get married than any time in the history of the United States. The average age for women's first marriage is now 27.1 years old and for men 29.1 years old. I spoke to a psychologist friend who has looked into the some of the reasons and agreed that these numbers are a bit surprising, but there are compelling reasons why they are true:

- More young people are going to college and it is so expensive they cannot afford the burden of a marriage until they become established in their careers.

- More women are graduating from college that ever before and are having careers.

- Those who have student loans feel really strapped for money and want to try to begin paying them off before getting married.

- More singles are living together to save money and avoid marriage and having children.

- People are having smaller families and having them later in life using planned parenthood.

- Average number of children per American women in marriage is now less than two. (Shocking! This is a very disturbing statistic; it means we are losing population)

Another somewhat negative cause and effect relationship seems to be how much change occurs in the two people after the couple does get married. The first year should be the time of the honeymoon, which may last the entire first year or end abruptly when the couple has their first big disagreement. Hopefully, they make up, become more aware of the other's feelings and needs, and move forward. The fact is people begin to change almost immediately after they begin living together. If both are conscientious and really want to make the marriage work and go smoothly, it may stay on an even keel for a while or even become stronger and more loving. Mutual love is the glue that binds two people together. When that is missing or dies out, the marriage is doomed. When one expects the other to be at their beck and call and do all the messy work, the marriage can get in trouble quickly. Today's women are much more independent not necessarily the way their mothers were and certainly not their grandmothers.

In trying to remain tactful, let's roll the calendar back at least 50 or 60 years and review some of the circumstances that existed then. A typical family had one car, mom stayed home, raised the kids, shopped once a week, walked a lot of places, did the laundry, kept the house, visited some with neighbors, wore a house dress, might go all day without makeup, and put up with a lot. The old television series, *The Honeymooners,* didn't miss the target by much and even *All in the Family,* with Archie Bunker, gave you a good glimpse at the family life of yesterday. I have news for you guys, that time is over for good, never to come again. Women are emancipated, are your equal, and many will not hesitate to tell you, so do not expect your marriage to be all about just your wants and needs. It will be about both your wants and needs and you must do your share. I really believe that not understanding, accepting, and living up to this balance is a large part of why marriages fail, especially if you have children early, which puts a lot of stress on a marriage. The second cause of collapsing marriages is not taking the marriage vows as the establishment of a sacred trust, a covenant between the two of you and God. God means for men and women to marry and have children and he does not intend for us to cast off our mate when things get a little uncomfortable or stressful.

Psychologists have a term called the seven-year itch. It marks the time when the happiness of a marriage may begin a decline that often results in one of the parties wanting to spice up his or her life and was ripe for an affair or diversion with someone new. It is not uncommon for a marriage to get stale. The problem today is that people are often far too willing to walk away from their marriage obligations and destroy most of their relationships instead of doing something to improve that relationship they already have. If you find yourself in this place, this book can help you re-balance your Life Circles and perhaps save a decaying marriage. People that are willing to throw in the towel obviously do not believe there is something worth saving about their marriage. I feel sorry for both parties because the spiritual side of their marriage never matured and at least one person does not regret the separation. Even when children are involved, they are willing to tear their little hearts in two for their own often selfish desires.

Because every marriage today has a 50-percent likelihood of ending in divorce, many people seem to become very disenchanted with their marriages earlier than ever before. The honeymoon for some doesn't last a year, let alone seven years before the itch begins. Assuming all this is true, one or both people in the marriage aren't really paying any attention to their vows. They just know they are supposed to say "I do" at the right time. Perhaps they just do not think about what they are getting into. This is my comment: in other words, you could assume from this analysis that the act of marriage ruins a perfectly good relationship. Does it somehow stifle the fun they have as singles? Is it avoiding responsibility that makes singles happy? This is quite scary. Has the devil taken over the institution of marriage? Are people becoming so spoiled to their uninhibited single lives that they can't put up with a little give and take?

I think a hidden reason for this may be that young people get accustomed to being in total control of their lives and are not willing to enter a marriage in which *negotiations* immediately begin dominating their lives together. I am sure the devil is pleased with the way marriage seems to be decaying, indicated by the number of divorces and broken homes that have resulted. But the worst dimension of this dilemma is the children who aren't sure who their daddy is anymore, or what it means to have a "family" they can count on, or a home where they can grow up without fear of losing it. The entire idea of making a lasting commitment is doing an exit-stage left.

Let me ask you a serious question. What does one spouse do when the other just casually tells him one evening while they are watching TV, "I wish I were not married to you because I don't love you, and I still love the last person I was married to and divorced 15 years ago and should never have divorced him?"

- First, you need to get over something in 15 years.

- Second, why wait until you are married again to decide something so damaging to your current marriage of 5 months?

- Third, you must have rehearsed this short speech several times before you destroyed your new husband by telling him this.

- Fourth, did you expect him to say, "Well that's okay, we'll just live together and see how you feel later?" At that moment he felt a switch turn off his love for her leaving nothing but shock and numbness.

- Fifth, did you expect him to be angry, is that what you wanted, or was it your attempt to crush him in one shot?

- Why would you be that mean when he had given you carte blanche to have and do whatever you wanted without constraints of any kind?

- What would you do in this circumstance?

This husband filed for an annulment and got it, but he was hurt psychologically and financially for a long time to come. Why did that confused and vindictive person ever agree to get married again in the first place if she had that kind of attachment in her past baggage? It beats me!

Dealing with situations like these in marriages today are one of the difficult parts of this book to write, because there are no right answers. There are observations you can make by being analytical but maybe we should think about how God feels. I think he may turn away from both parties in a divorce because he intended for us to select our mate, be faithful, and to love, honor, and to respect the other. When any of those elements goes away, especially love, then you are simply living in the same house and there is nothing left. It is then a sin to live together when no love is involved, and you are just going through the motions of trying to be polite to each other until one of the spouses moves out. The next things that happen are the two of you try to rebuild your separate lives and recover from the damage to families, friends, and relationships—some of which may never quite be the same again.

Some marriages end in divorce because there is no other solution, especially when love is gone. As Paul said in 1 Cor 13:11-14, "When I was a child, I spoke as a child, I understood as a child, I thought as a child, but now that I became a man, I put away childish things. For now we see in a mirror dimly but then face to face. Now I know in part, but then I shall know just as I also am known. And now abide faith, hope, love, these three, but the greatest is love." When love is gone, we have lost the most precious gift of all, because God is love. We disconnect from God and it will take a long winding road back to reconnect.

I really feel strongly that many single people today have a very false and childish idea of what marriage is all about. They aren't mature even though they are grown up physically; they are spoiled; they are used to instant gratification; they have not had enough hardship in their lives to build sufficient character to cope with the everyday challenges that they will face when married. If so, it is pathetic.

That is one reason why it is usually better if you have been divorced for a while and want to get married again, that you look for someone next time who has also been divorced for a while. At least the two of you should both have more realistic expectations, even though it does not always work.

There is what I call a psychic phenomenon with young people today that I call the "me first" or "I want it right now" syndrome. It comes from the media, commercials, ads, internet, numerous weekly publications, and the news that bombard us every day with outrageous promises of everything that will make us feel better and help us be more competitive, the best at whatever we do! We must be in front of the pack, leaders, number one. You can hardly enjoy a walk unless you are timing your pace on your wrist and trying to better what you did last time. Please don't fall into this trap, and if you have, climb back out, dust yourself off, and say, "Not me! Never again will I have to win at everything I do or worry about being Number One. I will be content to run with the pack. And I will be just as happy being a participant as the one who wins." You will be a lot happier person in the long run.

I think one reason God gave us different talents and abilities was so we could do some things very well naturally and not feel we have to be great at everything. Remember your mate will hopefully have talents you don't have and vice versa, so don't expect her or him to do what you do really well. Give each other breathing room. Do what you each enjoy and vice versa. That is what "give and take" is all about.

In other words, we are far too competitive, which worms its way into our marriages. We are expected to perform well in everything we do. And when we don't measure up, the spouse is disappointed and wants to throw us away and get a better one. No one seems to want to compromise to keep love alive.

Marriage takes work from both partners. When one shirks his or her responsibility, the other has to double up and after a while it gets old. If one mate spends lots of money every month and the other spends one tenth that amount, things are out of balance and will come crashing down. You would be advised to find out why this is happening and split your Family circle into his and her circles. Track things for a couple of months and have a sit-down discussion to get things back in balance. There can be reasons for this that are explainable, but if it is done essentially in secret, look out! Trouble is just around the corner. All big purchases should be done in the open and agreed to by both parties in advance. If balance cannot be resolved between the two people, the marriage is over and can't be fixed unless the big spender is cut off and made to realize he or she has serious problems.

You single people who are starting your adult life are being forewarned that your chance of having a lasting marriage is statistically about 50/50. Not a very happy number is it? What do I believe can raise that number in your favor? Before I try to answer that question, let me list a few prerequisites:

You both need to make your own list of likes and dislikes, personality traits, etc., but here are some ideas that may help you do that. Then sit down and discuss your lists with each other.

- Look for someone who has the same interests and tastes as you.

- Look for someone who likes to exercise 365 days a year, walking, running, sports, skiing, boating, swimming, at the gym, etc. Your Family and Friends circles will have a strong overlap with friends.

- Look for someone who has a similar background and upbringing as you who likes the same foods, likes to travel, likes animals (only if you like animals), is comfortable in a crowd, can entertain themselves without TV for a few hours or even all day, who likes to read, who talks to you without your having to start every conversation, is outgoing, and already has a lot of friends, not just a couple.

- Someone who insists on a pet the other does not want must assume full responsibility for its care, and even then it will certainly cause stress in the relationship.

- Someone who has a similar education.

- Someone who has a similar world view and faith in God and preferably worships as you do.

- Do not marry into a cult. If you were born into one, try your best to get out of it.

- Find someone who doesn't drink every day or need a drink to relax but isn't averse to a few drinks a week. The key is moderation and occasional.

- If you register well on all these things, you should have a much better probability of a good marriage when the time comes.

- You have to kiss a lot of frogs to find a prince or princess.

Simply put, look for a mate who is as compatible with your personality and background as you can find. If you lived in one part of the country all your life, think long and hard about marrying someone from another part of the country. It can work, but the transplanted person has to make a big effort adapting to the new culture. I did that once and it was an eye-opening experience and true culture shock. The one I lived through ended badly 11 years later.

If you rush through a short engagement, you will have a much harder time evaluating all the quirks and habits the other person has that could be serious negatives. A counselor I admire for her good judgment and advice recommends that a couple agree to be engaged for a year and go through all four seasons together. She says you will learn so much about each other during that time that your final decision will be much better grounded. Carolyn and I went through a long-distance courtship and engagement for over a year and we got to know and depend on each other during that time. We also ran up some enormous phone bills talking almost every night. In those days, there was no such thing as toll-free calling anywhere in the United States. We always jokingly told people we had to get married to stop our $500 monthly phone bills.

You must realize that many people get married because it is expected of them by their families, friends, your girlfriend or boyfriend, etc. If your priority is more education, a more challenging job, leaving the country for a while to see the world and perhaps work someplace, or for whatever reason you prefer to remain single, then I applaud your decision. Go do it, follow your heart and don't be surprised if you mature a great deal from the experience.

If a friend you left behind is still around when your wanderlust is over, you might renew your relationship. Just remember to make new friends wherever you go, enjoy your life, and keep looking for the purpose that God has for you. You will know it when you find it because it will satisfy that inward craving you have. It could be a job where you can help people. And, remember most people have more than one talent, so try to figure out what you really enjoy doing, and then try to figure out how to make a living doing it. God will be pleased.

6

Coping With Young Children

AFTER GETTING MARRIED, MOST couples decide when they want to start a family. On average, this time is shifted later in their lives then it once was. Modern families often wait until the couple is in their 30s, which allows time for them to establish their home, save a little money, become comfortable with each other, and have stable employment.

Conversely, there are still young people who get out of high school and cannot wait to get married and don't seem to care about the risks that follow that thinking. If this is you and it is working well for you, congratulations and more power to you. That was more or less the convention when I grew up and got married the first time, and we did well for about 10 years before it began to disintegrate, and then it wasn't getting married too young that was the cause of our breakup. So, I will never tell you it's wrong to marry so young.

I know several couples from high school who married and have had strong life-long marriages. I believe the secrets in their successes were strong compatibility and a powerful desire to make it work. One couple had dated in high school and knew each other well, had a lot of mutual friends, their parents were supportive, and maybe two other things they had in common, they loved each other deeply and they loved God and their church. They had a great marriage.

So, regardless of how old the couple is, there is a list of prerequisites for starting the family at an opportune time when all the other life forces seem to be going along smoothly. It helps if the woman's mother lives in the same general area as the couple because she is going to be needed. In the ideal world, the couple is successful, and the woman gets pregnant with minimum complications and the first child comes into the world. The day she goes into labor their world turns upside down and everything in their lives is suddenly different. After the baby comes home, the husband begins learning a lot of things like disposable diapers come in several sizes, and if a bottle is involved, there is a lot of preparation required every day for the next year. And suddenly laundry has to be done a lot more often and with gentle soap and conditioner and there is a myriad of little details that are required almost continuously. The husband must remember to be very nice and patient, and not to get upset about things like stopping up the toilet by accidentally flushing a dirty diaper that gets stuck.

It is a good idea for the husband to take at least a week or two off from work to help his wife. Some companies offer the benefit of a paternity leave for new fathers. Meanwhile, someone must cook and shop for groceries and things that babies need. Hopefully, her mother can be called upon to help and it will be the best help you can find anywhere.

I spoke to a new father the other night who looked haggard, and I asked, "How is it going?" He replied, "the baby won't sleep at night and keeps us both up and then sleeps all day. I am about to lose my mind." I replied, "Welcome to fatherhood. It will get better, so hang in there. Just try to sleep anytime and anywhere you can for a few days and try to keep the baby up when it is light outside."

My experience was raising four children and having them survive to become responsible adults, which does not make me an expert by any stretch of my imagination, but I know what to expect and how to survive. Some women spend an hour in delivery, while others go through a very difficult delivery and are worn out by the trauma, so be extra helpful and nice. Their energy levels are generally very low for the first week after delivery. Each successive child is easier, mostly because you know better what to expect.

So, you have your first child, and learn a lot by doing and listening to your mother and friends with children. There are a few good books which your Pediatrician can recommend. In 1943, Dr.

Spock came on the scene, and his eighth revision *Dr. Spock's Baby and Child Care*, is an informative book. He died in 1998, in his 90s, but his ideas are still pretty much mainstream. I believe that when children are small is the most challenging time in their lives and those of the parents.

From this point forward, you need to look at your Life Circles periodically to check their balance. The last thing you need to do with a toddler of maybe two years old is to begin building a larger Friends circle for yourself that takes away from your Family circle. That little toddler needs Mommy and Daddy more than ever and will continue to need you as he or she grows to begin pre-school and then elementary school. If you have another baby in the next few years, the demands on you will continue to increase. At the last comprehensive census, American families on average are down to 1.5 children, which means we are losing population over time, which is a sad as well as serious situation.

As a couple, you won't have much discretionary time till your kids get into school, or perhaps pre-school. It is certainly an appropriate time to introduce the date night idea I talked about in Chapter 4, where you and your wife get a sitter and go out to dinner or a movie or whatever you want to do to get away for a few hours. Mothers of the couple make the best first baby sitters. Preteens from the neighborhood do not make good sitters for infants because they simply do not have enough experience to know what to do if the baby chokes or won't quit crying.

A key question in today's society: Does the wife in this discussion have a career that she wants to re-start after having each child? Two incomes may sound good initially, but do you really want someone else to raise your children? That is a very hard decision that should not be made lightly.

I have rather negative feelings about it and didn't want my wife to go back to work, nor did she after we were married, and she loved being at home. She had worked her entire adult life and was relieved not to have to work even when things were rough financially. It let her do things like being a homeroom mother, Welcome Wagon lady, deliver Meals on Wheels for many years, creative things like painting, a women's club with her friends, decorate and work doing the bulletin in the early days of our church, and set up a free Christmas store for several years for 40 poor children to pick out a present for free and wrap them for their mothers (and some for grandmothers). She organized and ran all the holiday parties for them as well for several years. She made and took meals to people in need, and sent cards and notes to sick, shut-ins, and people in assisted living. She epitomized what a good friend should be.

So, when deciding to be a working spouse, there is no right or wrong answer; it depends greatly on the spouse's personality, ambition, and desire to do benevolent things, and still meet the needs of the children. Some children are needier than others. I have recently encountered a couple of Mr. Moms, who run their homes and take care of their young children. Obviously, her job was better and/or paid more than his and they made the switch.

Whether the young mother works or not, I believe that church-run day care and preschool classes are a wonderful thing for the children to attend. Ours went to these; it cures shyness if they would otherwise be alone with a sitter or their mothers or grandparents, it encourages interaction with other children and communication skills, and teaches them to play, learn and sing songs, and to get along with others. Our church runs one and to look in at them having lunch is a wonderful experience. They are all so cute and so well behaved it amazes me. Our lady workers do an incredible job with them.

My daughters should be writing this chapter and for sure I will solicit their review and comments, making sure I don't go too far counter-culture. I will be rude from the beginning and take a shot at those who never correct or lift a finger to their precious little tyke's fanny when he or she is screaming his or her head off being wheeled through a mall or store or sitting in a restaurant. Nor am I in favor of being too strict, but the pendulum has swung too far to the "indulge your children" side of the discipline scale. I also want to ask the parents whose children are well behaved what their secret is. Do they ever discipline their children? And if so, how? I'd be interested in recording their replies.

I think the most important thing is not to lose you temper with your children. I remember as a child something that I think is the wrong way to handle punishing a child, and it was the way a lot of us were raised when I was young. If you did something your mother didn't like, her immediate response was to scold me and say, "You just wait till your father gets home." Well, the rest of my day was ruined, and I moped around waiting for the official spanking from my father. One day when my father came home he took me out to the coal shed and looked at me and said, "I am done with these spankings when I come home. If your mother wants to spank you she can, but I am not going to do it anymore when I come home. It ruins my night and yours too." That was the end of my spankings. Maybe I wised up at that moment.

There are times when I know I was asleep in Parenting 101 and missed a lot of opportunities to do the right thing raising my children, but my wife Carolyn was there to set me straight, and to her I give all the accolades for how they turned out. She taught me at least two things that stuck, and these were: always give your children unconditional love and do what your instinct tells you to do. I believe that women in general have better intuition in raising children than men. It's the bond in the womb that links their lives in a way that fathers don't have.

The next few paragraphs cover some really disquieting news that new parents should know. To begin, here also are two factoids I think are important. First, years ago Dr. James Dobson noted that 70 percent of our traits and personality are inherited. Second, genetic studies at University of Minnesota concluded that some babies come into the world looking for a fight. These babies are strong-willed and want things their way, and you must patiently teach them that they are not the boss. From other genetic studies, there are more bad genes than there used to be, mostly because we are poisoning our planet at an alarming rate with careless use of plastics, tobacco, numerous chemicals, food additives, manu-factured and genetically modified seeds and foods, all sorts of pollution, and overprescribed pharmaceuticals, to name the worst offenders.

From these three disconnected observations, I conclude that it will be more difficult for today's babies to grow up to be healthy, normal, well behaved, and well adjusted than ever before. Conversely, mortality rates for newborns and infants continue to decline because expectant mothers get much better care than in the past, but once these children begin to be exposed to all the bad elements in the environment and food chain, there is an increase in childhood diseases, with new ones continuing to pop up that are more difficult to treat.

Day care is a good place for the little ones to begin their collection of antibodies because little kids tend to freely share their germs. Do not be surprised if your little ones get some strange illnesses, but taking them to pre-school is worth a few trips to the doctor because of all the positive learning they experience. In addition, pre-school builds their antibodies and makes them healthier children than kids that stay shut in too much.

In my opinion, you should work at becoming a decent cook, do as much as you can yourself, and leave as much prepared food as possible at the market and the fast-food stores. This explains the popularity of Organic foods. They really help. In Spring and Summer, try growing your own garden vegetables in dirt you know has not been treated with herbicides and use only organic fertilizer. Do everything you can to eliminate foods with artificial food coloring, which is one of the worst of all food additives and is in everything. Why is this such a common practice? I don't know. Become a label reader.

Sorry to go on a tear, but people need to know that raising children is harder in some respects today than it was when I was a child. It is harder because there are many more ways you can screw it up unless you know better and are proactive when feeding your family. So, the more knowledge you have in the beginning, the better off you and your children will be. When I was young, there were no prepared meals you could buy at the super market and no fast food stores, and you could ask the butcher for a ham bone or a bone for your dog. Everything came wrapped in paper or cardboard and was biodegradable. Our choices were much more limited but somehow Mother always made it taste great except for cabbage, which she always cooked to mush.

Like all other children when I was young, I am sure I had large Family and Self circles. The Self circle is what makes us individuals and sets us apart from all other people. It defines our wants, needs, loves, passions, talents, experiences, tastes, personality, and even that secret place our mind wanders, our imagination. Self is by nature selfish: it allows us to be whatever we want to be, do whatever we want to do, and to become the person we are as we grow up. Self should be ruled by the conscience but is often ruled by desire. Look out for the "I want it now," instant gratification, whatever "it" happens to be.

Something else I have noticed is the difference in raising one child vs. two or more children. My oldest daughter has one child, who is 21 and finishing up his degree. He has a great personality and is very talented in music, plays several instruments and has even played with a local symphony Orchestra. Our younger daughter came along 14 years after her sister, so we were single parents for several years and then had two, and then the older daughter went away to school and got married, and we were back with one child to raise.

The dynamic of raising a single child is a lot different from raising two. Our youngest daughter has two girls two years apart and they have very different personalities, both great kids, both competitive, both can put on an impromptu play and act out a dialogue with no coaching, sing the same songs, and are both adorable. They are now 12 and 14. What I noticed is that when it is one, as a parent you are much more indulgent than when there are two. As parents of one, you are involved with them much more every day; two entertain themselves much more, whereas one must be busy doing something and having friends over and be on the go constantly.

So how soon do we begin discussing God and Jesus to our children? Even when our children are very young we must teach them to listen to their conscience and not do things they know are bad or wrong. It is not ever too young to introduce the idea of God and

Jesus into the lives of our little children, which is another reason church-run day care and preschool are so beneficial. They reinforce God and Jesus in children's lives when they are in this most receptive period.

When the little ones are going to bed and hopefully to sleep, a short prayer is an effective way to begin this process. God bless Mommy and Daddy and grandparents and all the things they remember. They are usually attached to one soft stuffed animal or doll and they can bless it too. I can remember being upset when I was little by the line "if I should die before I wake, I pray the Lord my soul to take." I finally told my mother not to say that anymore. Good night prayers should be sweet without threats of death. That is really heavy. I never taught that one to my kids. A much better idea is to softly sing *"Jesus loves me"* to them. Remember, they are totally reliant on their parents when very young and should be taught as many pleasant things as possible, which they absorb like a sponge. I might add some of the children's stories and even some nursery rhymes I remember were awful and unnecessarily gruesome. The Brothers Grimm certainly were just that.

In a personal trip down memory lane, some of my earliest memories are of Sunday School and my teacher, Miss Ellie, who loved us all and taught us about God and Jesus. We would always sing songs and say little short prayers, and she taught us about "self-control." It got hammered into all of us. As a result, I grew up in the church and was an acolyte and later became a Lay Reader and made several life-long friends. It was an important and very nice part of growing up.

I felt the Holy Spirit sort of merged with my conscience and helped guide my life until about age 17 when I guess I believed I was ready to face life head on and forgot to continue to use God as my autopilot. For me, it was the age of rebellion and my parents didn't know what to do with me, so they tried to crack down on me more and more, and I resisted more and more. I wanted more than anything else to be 21 and on my own, and I didn't handle the next 5 or 6 years well at all, but that is another story that I recited in the early part of Chapter 3.

Just remember at bedtime all children (and spouses, too) need to feel safe and above all, loved. So, tell them you love them every day and especially every night at bedtime. All children love to hear bedtime stories especially about when you were young. You should always give them a happy ending even if you have to get a bit creative.

7

Mid-Life Couples With Children

SOME OF YOU ARE still in the military active reserves and must go to places like Afghanistan, placing your life in jeopardy and on hold while your spouses stay back with the children and worry about you every moment of every day. I admire your service and salute you. You are the backbone of America's defensive forces.

First, a good news story. Men, and sometimes women, this is the time in your life when you are hitting your stride in your work and earning enough to be relatively comfortable unless perhaps you swallowed too big a mortgage and have too many payments every month. Let's assume, for the most part you are doing at least okay and are hopefully sound financially, and your kids are nearing or have reached adolescence. In short, they are now old enough for you to leave them at home by themselves and you have tested them enough to know they are responsible and careful with the house, etc.

These should be some of the best years of your life because you are usually in good health, can do almost anything you want to do, go almost anywhere you want on vacation, live it up a little, eat out when the mood strikes you and generally enjoy your prosperity. To me, this model family is also a spiritual family that believes they owe some of the good life to God's blessings and, in response, attend a religious service regularly. In this model for most Americans, this is a church.

Jeff Walling, an author and preacher of some renown, came to speak at our church one Sunday at least 20 years ago and what he said made such a lasting impression on me that I wrote it down and saved it for all these years. He said, "There are three kinds of people: strong believers, luke-warm believers, and non-believers." He said, "give me the first and the third, but deliver me from the second. They are really hard people to reach because they think they are doing everything right and most of what I say never penetrates their insulation."

If these people have a Spiritual circle, which I have yet to discuss because I am saving it for Chapter 10, it would be tiny by comparison to all the other Life Circles, because it only gets a few hours a week devoted to it. Stay tuned for "The Rest of the Story," a term coined by commentator Paul Harvey years ago. I will let the cat's head out of the bag just enough to tell you that you cannot have a religious relationship with your God on a part-time Sunday and maybe Wednesday night basis. It is just not enough. It must be there when you wake up every morning and be there when you go to bed at night and remain with you as you go through every day of your life. It must help guide your decisions every day and you need to be aware that God's glory is there in front of you always. You must be grateful and in awe of God every day. As you love and worship God in this manner, He will in turn love you more.

You show God you love him when you do good things for other people, have relationships that last, and do charitable deeds. Once you embrace God this way, it affects how you treat you children, your mate, your friends, your work, your church family, and everyone you meet every day. It makes you a more likeable, thoughtful, and generous person. It makes you feel better about everything you do. When you reach this level of spiritual maturity, your marriage will be stronger and more able to accept the disappointments and hardships that come on occasion, because you know that God is with you to help you cope.

So, to summarize, there are millions of families out there across the world that are strong believers, that look to God for advice through the Holy Spirit, that have discovered that it is more rewarding to give and help others than to receive, and who live daily by His word. Strive to be one of these families and work at it because sometimes it will not be easy. Making the effort is worth it.

The chapter will affect many of you who read this book because it is your age-group that has the biggest problems with divorce, and are most likely to find your marriage is not what it should be. Something is missing. Sometimes it is hard to figure out why your mate is not as attractive to you or attracted to you as he or she once was. Perhaps you are both aware that your intimate moments are farther apart and lack the same spark they once had, or you are running your legs off every day with kids' events, school, sports events and practices, and you just don't feel like being lovey. Or the husband's job is really getting to him. You and your mate are in a rut. Examine your Life Circles and see if you can spot the problem. This is the period where most divorces incubate and then burst into the open and it is usually too late when that happens. If your marriage is worth saving, let's stop that from happening! The next example brings home the point.

The Work and Family circles often tend to become opposing forces like the poles of a magnet, so what is good for the family is often a detractor from your work, and vice versa. However, when managed properly, you can have good results in both circles. I must admit, I am far from perfect myself in reaching a good balance, but at least I am not blind to my shortcomings and I try to compensate, although often imperfectly and sometimes too late. As a couple grows together and has children, there are often times when you must sacrifice one circle for the other, and instead of your and your mate's circles being in harmony (close to being the same), they go far out of balance. When this happens, they set up opposing forces and become destructive.

My worst personal failure occurred when I put the job first, I left my wife with a 4-month old baby and a 14-year-old with unfulfilled obligations and went off to California to manage a new project my company had just won. One evening, my wife was fixing supper and realized she was missing a key ingredient, ran to the store two blocks away, but forgot to turn off the grease in a frying pan on the stove. It erupted in flames minutes later. Our 14-year-old's quick thinking saved the house and baby, she dumped baking soda and salt on the fire, but the kitchen had to be replaced and we had a lot of smoke damage. That was an awful time for us and my boss couldn't understand why I wanted to be replaced and return home. He reminded me several times what a bad career decision that was. I learned the hard way to put my family's needs first, and no job is more important. I left California the next day and we spent a lot of time struggling to put our life back in balance.

If your life circles are essentially balanced with a decent amount of cross-over coupling between Family and Friends circles, plan a date night and get out of the house together. Have a nice dinner and glass of wine and talk about it to see if he or she has something bothering them that they have been reluctant to discuss. If so, get it out on the table. Try to be a good listener and tell your partner you miss the closeness you once had, and you want to rekindle the fire. Tell him or her how much he or she means to you and ask about needs or wants. Sometimes it's a simple fix, while other times it will take some work; but fixing something that has put up a wall between you and your spouse is worth the effort.

Since date night is an important event, plan something exciting for the next one, like dancing or a club or perhaps a microbrewery that has entertainment. Go to a show you both want to see and try to get some excitement back into the relationship. You may go out with other couples if it has been a while since you did that. Three or even four couples can make a fun night. Plan to do something together. If you have been doing a lot of separate activities, that in itself may be part of the feeling of emptiness in your relationship—that feeling that he or she isn't paying attention to me anymore! Plan a weekend trip together to places you haven't been in long time. Kick back and embrace each other and have some fun, leaving all your problems back at home.

My wife and I would go to a small town high in the mountains of North Carolina called Highlands for long weekend trips. It claims to be the highest incorporated town East of the Mississippi River with great food, excellent accommodations, lots of specialty shops, very friendly people, and lots of sidewalk benches where you can strike up a conversation anytime you want. Remember, I said you have to "stop and smell the roses every so often" elsewhere in this book, and I truly believe God rejoices when we enjoy nature, beautiful waterfalls and scenery, and give ourselves a break from the routine. It is restorative and good for the soul. I sometimes think it gives us a tiny glimpse of what heaven may be like. The same is true of going to the beach; it, too, is very restorative. I can stare at the ocean for hours on end and never get weary of it. Both are wonderful places to see God's work in abundance. Of course, it is everywhere, and you just have to open your eyes. Some people look through the windshield and see only the cars ahead and the road; I see the panorama of God's handiwork.

Sometimes putting the spotlight on a relationship is a tremendous help if there is something else going on that you don't know about. If there is, it is likely to expose that something if it does exist, and it may not be too late to do something about it.

Even some things that seem completely terrible, such as a brief affair that can wreck a marriage, can be forgiven and dealt with, and the marriage saved if the offending party is truly repentant and wants to be forgiven. Assuming the couple once had a strong relationship, perhaps until the children came along, and they had what could be considered strong mutual love, give it another chance. Sometimes there are still enough glowing coals to rekindle the fire. Don't give up too easily. If it is something less serious, see if you two can talk it out and resolve it, and then make up for the time you lost being distant and reclusive. Don't keep things inside, because that is where they fester and get magnified out of proportion.

It is a lot better for the children and both of you in the long run to salvage a marriage than to get a divorce. Consult with friends who got divorces (and perhaps some that didn't) and listen to their stories. They often regret doing it too quickly, but it got so nasty (mostly because of opposing lawyers' interference) that it got out of control and they couldn't fix it in time. That is why in some states, a no-fault divorce seems so silly and yet it is why they have a waiting period of 2 years to see if the parents will reconcile. What did they really have wrong with their marriage that couldn't have been fixed? And do they realize what psychological damage they do to their children? Hardly ever. Of course, to stay in a broken relationship in the same house is also just as damaging to the children because they don't know if mom and dad are okay with each other or not. If your marriage has to end, so be it. Some of the finest people I have ever known came from broken homes. They made steadfast friends and understood people's problems more acutely because of their firsthand experiences.

Now let's discuss some bad situations. I present four scenarios for your consideration. When I asked a few friends to review this book before it was complete, one reviewer said these examples made her very sad. I certainly agree. Divorce is a sad experience, made much worse when there are children involved. It hurts many people, leaves deep emotional damage regardless of who is at fault, and it can destroy people financially just to name a few consequences. The main reason for using these examples is to remind some of you readers that divorce is serious and has lasting consequences, and even if you think it will solve your problems, it may not.

Scenario 1: This story is one in which the husband and wife disagreed vehemently over how to raise the children, but it could be almost any reason for disagreement. The husband was always on their backs fussing and bullying them. Thus, the children were caught in the middle, and there was a lot of yelling at the kids and the husband threatened his wife physically, browbeat, and intimidated her because he was bigger and stronger than she was. This marriage ended in a messy divorce in which she had to have a restraining order served against her ex.

At some point could it have been saved? Only if the husband was willing to seek professional help, and with his temperament, the odds were against him from the start. Any husband that threatens or does physical harm to his wife is a hard person to save. He has serious personality issues and often mental problems. Or as my father would have said, "He is just a mean person." There are some people who were abused, perhaps from early childhood, and as adults, they want to take it out on everyone around them. You see their pictures in the Post Office and on TV.

When you find situations like this, you ask yourself how and why did these two ever get married in the first place? It was clearly a mistake and people who knew them saw they would have problems as soon as the husband didn't get his way all the time, as well as everything he wanted out of the marriage. Selfish people on either side of a marriage make very bad mates. I ask you a simple question: where is God in these kinds of marriages? I think God is with the wife, but I don't know about the husband. Jesus warned us that he may not know us if we fall away too far.

In this scenario, the wife somehow put her life back together and survived being a single provider with children to raise. Nothing is much worse, and this country is full of people who have similar stories. I prayed that her church would understand that she had no choice for her own sake and that of her children, and would be understanding, kind, and helpful. In another case where something very similar happened close to me, the parents of the mother were her life savers. This is often the case and it all came out okay years later, but it was very hard on the mother to survive at the time it was happening. Her close friends also came to her rescue on many occasions.

Scenario 2: The wife and husband both work but she has assigned shifts that vary week to week, which turns out convenient for her to dodge her family responsibilities. Thus, the father being a nice guy, takes on the role of taking their two kids to school, church, shopping, and meeting their friends, etc. Between working full time and being a surrogate mother, the husband is tapped out. Little does he know that the wife has a boyfriend and is living the free-style life she always wanted. When it all comes out in the open, the wife fights the husband tooth and nail for custody and the kids want to live with their daddy, and it gets really ugly after that. A couple of years go by, their divorce is final, but the custody trials drag on forever.

Who wins in this case? You pray the judge has enough sense to study the case file and grant the husband custody, but old precedence dies hard and the woman usually gets what she wants, as sad as this situation is. Cases like this continue to do damage to the children and parents. The only sensible solution is for the parents to stop fighting and let one parent have the responsibility of raising the children until they are in their mid-to-late teen when they are old enough to decide their own fate.

Scenario 3: The husband announces one day he is leaving and he packs up and is gone. In these cases, they usually say, "I don't love you anymore and we have nothing in common, so I am leaving." The wife is standing there with her mouth open wondering what she did wrong to make this happen. So, she vacillates between getting angry and blaming herself for his misdeeds. I estimate 90 percent of the time, the husband in these situations has a younger girlfriend and has been sneaking around with her. Certainly, for the injured party, these separations are among the most common and the most devastating for the wife, who now has the sole responsibility for the children and is usually the least capable of coping with the financial burden it creates.

Incidentally, these separations fall into two categories, ones in which the family was well off financially, and those in which the wife is left with very little and has to return to work if she wasn't working at the time. If she were, she is a little better off but her standard of living is about to take a severe nosedive. Child care suddenly becomes her primary concern, and can she afford to keep her home intact, or will she have to sacrifice that as well? She is devastated and if their marriage was their first and one in which they had all their children, then she is likely to need two things immediately—a good divorce attorney, and possibly a counselor to help her cope with all the feelings and emotions she has a result.

In this scenario, the couple have grammar school children, but his income was not enough to support two houses and the family he left behind. She hires a lawyer to seek support for herself and her children, and things get even uglier because everything then goes through the lawyer and enormous amounts of time and money are wasted, especially affecting the injured party, who cannot afford it. She soon runs out of money, so she goes back to work and then has the problem of day care. Her family and some friends help her some, but she is still suffering greatly, along with the self-doubts. Her self-esteem plunges.

She doesn't see how she will ever recover from this terrible setback in her life and that of her children. To make matters worse, the errant husband, faced with big bills for child support and alimony, skips town and is yet to be found. Florida was once the state that had no extradition for runaway husbands. I knew one personally who had abandoned his wife and children and paid them no support while he was living comfortably with another woman in Florida, with no intention of ever leaving the state.

My personal note to the wife in this scenario is that somehow you will eventually overcome because you cannot let your children down, and with the help of friends and your job, you will persevere and become a stronger person than you ever imagined you could be. God is with you and you must keep your faith strong and feel His presence in your life. Many people are praying for you.

Scenario 4: The wife calls the husband one morning when he is at work and says she is leaving, and her husband asks, "Where are you going?" and she says, "I'm leaving you. The kids are in day care, so pick them up by 3 o'clock, goodbye!" She then hangs up. That will ruin your morning. This was before cell phones. So, the husband picked up the kids and went home to find her closet and dresser empty. She had run off with her man friend who left his wife the same day and they both did the same thing to their mates.

About a year later, the husband still has the kids, sells his house and downsizes and moves to where he can find better day care and support, and runs the family. His wife calls him one day, crying and wanting to come back and be their mother again. She misses the children terribly and wants to work things out with him. He, like a fool, accepts her story and tells her to come back. The next day he gets up and goes to work because he has missed so many days and has no more time off. He comes home all happy with expectations of a reconciliation and finds the locks on all the doors have been changed and he can't get into his own house. Through the door she cries out, "I fooled you. It's my house now, and I'll call the cops and have you arrested if you don't leave now."

The husband spent the night in a motel and she had the upper hand from then on.

She had no intention of ever making up with him and tricked him very effectively. "She got the gold mine and he got the shaft." After four court trials, the final ruling was she got custody of both children and he got to pay all the bills. She got his house, a car, medical care, and child support for years after. And she had walked out on him and left her kids! Sometimes there isn't much justice in the legal system. A few weeks after occupying the house, she enrolled them in school under the last name of her man friend even though she wasn't even divorced until two years later. That really hurt the husband's legacy when his only heirs disappeared from all records. Although the entire story came out in court, the judge wasn't listening and had already made up her mind that the wife would get everything, ignoring all evidence that led up to that point, such as her desertion of her children in the first place.

My advice on this one is do not fall victim to an errant spouse who suddenly wants to make up with you; do not let them back into your house and force it to take time to evolve into something genuine and not a clever masquerade. The husband really got taken to the cleaners, financially as well as psychologically. His children were later separated from him geographically by a thousand miles, which resulted in inconvenient and expensive visitation and some measure of alienation. It was a difficult situation for the children and their father.

If we are any student of the Bible, we are taught that divorce is a sin. We are also taught that Jesus died on the cross for our sins and therefore cleared the path for sinners to inherit the kingdom of heaven if we believe in him and confess our sins and ask for forgiveness. The third point is that all sins are bad. Those called out in the Ten Commandments are more serious sins, the ones God gave to Moses, and divorce is not one of them. I know divorce is a sin, but I believe Jesus will forgive a divorce that has a valid reason, and further, I believe that when love truly dies in a marriage that it is more of a sin to stay together than to separate. Because God is love, if people stay together without love, they are denying God in their lives, and that is a very serious sin.

I also believe that the scenarios I discussed above are all too common examples of situations that merit divorce, that couldn't be saved because one of the parties broke their sacred vows to love, honor and respect the other person. Nor was the person who left their spouse in these situations one bit remorseful about what they did. They typically say they had to leave to keep their sanity because their spouse was driving them crazy. When you destroy the love in the marriage by your actions, it is extremely doubtful that marriage can be saved. Even when a couple believes they can reconcile a broken marriage, will the deep trust and unconditional love that existed before in their marriage ever return? If it does, then they can possibly save it; if not, it isn't worth trying.

8

Empty Nesters

COUPLES WHO NO LONGER have children at home are the focus of this chapter, not necessarily older couples that I cover in the next chapter under Retirement. Well more than half the empty nesters are still working and not ready to retire, not yet on Social Security, and have rich and vibrant lives. They usually have a bit more money that the mid-life couples who are raising their children in Chapter 7.

First, let us talk about some good things that happen to empty nesters. They usually have added resources that younger people do not have, because they typically keep a large enough house for the children and grandchildren to come back to at Christmas and other holidays, vacations, etc. I still maintain a 4-bedroom house and do not venture upstairs where three of those bedrooms are except to clean and dust occasionally, look for a book or tax records and maybe change the thermostat seasonally. I suppose I believe it is a little perk I keep so the kids will always have a place to come home to. I am also a sentimental sort of person, and the bedrooms are named for the children. One of my daughters only recently asked for a piece of furniture from her bedroom for a larger home she is remodeling and yet to move into. I was glad she asked.

If you are an empty nester, does some of this resonate with you? My wife and I always tended to be people who didn't throw things away, so year-to-year, the upstairs stays the same. Maybe it also adds to my comfort, but I have thought about downsizing. What would I do with all that stuff (my collective name for everything upstairs)? It is all so new-looking and under-used; it stays nice. Maybe I need to find someone who needs a fully furnished house. Oh well, I probably won't downsize this year. I may think about it again, but not too seriously.

Getting back to the issue of Life Circles, as long as I continue work some, my Work, Family, and Friends circles are all three about the same size, and my Self circle is a little smaller than the others. However, I do a lot of introspection when I write, so mine may be larger than some of yours. If you are a true empty nester, please give your circles another look and change their sizes as necessary. To qualify, you once had children and they now have their own homes and families. It may not be necessary to tweak the size of your circles. You are blessed if your children are still in the same geographic area as you so they can drop in and vice versa; mine both live in different states, which can be extremely inconvenient.

Now let's focus on your Friends circle. It reflects on how active you are, how often you interact with and spend time with your friends, and how coupled are both of you are to your friends. Do you take trips together sometimes, see each other frequently, eat at each other's houses, etc.? Or, conversely, are most of these friends yours and then your mate has his or hers? I mentioned earlier that God encourages us to have lasting, healthy relationships. Are most of these friends of both you and your mate or do you go your separate ways quite a bit, and if this is the case, are you both happy with how it works week to week? If you discuss this issue openly with your wife and she is even the least bit negative, try to determine if this needs to be rebalanced.

As empty nesters, do you travel more and have more free time, or has work got you a little too dominated? If the latter is the case, you might consider doing something about it. If it is causing you unnecessary stress, you should definitely do something about it before your health is affected. Personally, I did not heed these warning signs soon enough even though I realized how stressful the job was and ended up with a heart bypass the year I gave up that job.

Talk about a life changer, a bypass will do it. That and a heart attack are the two biggest wake-up calls you will ever get, and they are mostly unnecessary if you listen to your inner self; it knows when you are crossing the line, and your Life Circles will also tell you. But I thought I was the picture of health and able to do everything I attempted, so I ignored the warning signs. I survived the operation just fine and continue to exercise regularly. It also made me appreciate my family, friends, and spiritual life a lot more.

This period in your lives gives you great opportunities to see the world, take both ocean and river cruises (with or without other couples), see the beautiful places in the U.S., perhaps buy a beach or vacation home, and kick back and enjoy life more. It also gives you opportunities to do more significant charity and benevolent work. This is a good time to pick the things that mean the most to you and your family, and then get involved with a significant effort. You will be rewarded in many ways and you will be pleasing God.

These are your golden years, so take advantage while you can. I have always enjoyed the bumper sticker on the back of many motorhomes that reads, "We are spending our kids inheritance." Pretty funny and true. Travel can give you a lot of opportunities to meet a lot of very nice people.

I must tell you about my wife and my last trip to Maine about four years ago. We had been to Booth Bay some years earlier and were there for the final evening band concert of the season. When they played in the open air, it was an incredibly emotional experience with lots of patriotic songs, so we agreed to come back again someday; thus we returned four years ago and stayed at a nice hotel on the East side of the bay.

This time, we arrived too late in the season for the band concert, but the hotel had a raised fire pit, which turned into a favorite meeting place. For three nights in a row, we had great conversations with people from all over the country. The amazing thing was that the first night, a couple was there from New Jersey, and he mentioned where he worked. It was where I had worked years earlier, and we had the same boss, so my wife and I said later, "What are the chances are of that happening?" So, the next night, we went back to the fire pit and nothing happened for a little while. Then, a new couple walked up, and we made introductions. I asked where they were from and he said Atlanta, so I asked if he knew a friend of ours who was in the same line of work as he was and went to our church. It turned out they had worked together often and he had met with them recently. So, my wife and I said, "This is just getting to be too weird and it could never happen again." So, our last night there, we went back to the fire pit and the couple in the next room came down. They said they had heard us talking and recognized my wife's accent; they were from Mobile. They always helped to put on Mobile's Mardi Gras Parade, so I asked if they knew a past King and Queen who had run around with us before they moved to Mobile, and he said they were good friends. Three for three is amazing!

I ask you, what are the odds that we could do that three nights in a row in Booth Bay Harbor, Maine? The point in telling this story is that empty nesters can and do have experiences like this. You must be willing to make the first move, open the conversation, and you will almost always have something in common with most people you meet. God wants us to interact with people and I thoroughly enjoy doing it. Being friendly and outgoing are two very good traits to cultivate. God loves relationships; they are part of his plan for us here on earth.

We know at least five couples who have traveled all over the US in big motor homes and have left friends wherever they stopped for any length of time. One couple's motor home broke down in Wyoming or Montana in some sparsely populated place and after talking to a family they met by going to a little church they found, were invited to stay with them, which they did until the parts finally arrived and were installed. I would call that the extreme case, but it really happened. This proves there are good people everywhere you go in this great country of ours. When you reach empty nester status, get adventurous. You will be glad you did, and it may be you who has to initiate the conversations, but it can be exceedingly rewarding.

I remember one instance in Concord, New Hampshire when my wife and I both needed our hair cut, so we walked into a barber shop on the main street and the barber assured us that he could do both, so before we sat down, we commented on his sign that said,

"Home of the $400 Haircut." He had blowups of all the primary candidates' checks for $400 on the walls of his shop. Because the New Hampshire Caucus is the first primary in the nation, and after candidate John Edwards got his $400 haircut (circa 2007) from a famous stylist and became the laughing stock of the nation, this barber offered to give each candidate a $400 haircut, but for charity. The idea took off, he collected a lot of money for charity, and he had a lot of fun doing it. Every candidate gave him a check except John Edwards, who by then gave up trying to get nominated. We found everyone we met in New England very friendly and some quite humorous.

I highly recommend a charity that takes some of your time on a regular basis. As long as you are in good health, things like Meals on Wheels, tutoring, or helping at a center for underprivileged children, driving people without transportation to doctor visits, picking up or shopping for people who can't get out or can't drive, are but a few volunteer things you can do that please God. He really expects you to do these kinds of things because he loves it when you are a servant. He sent Jesus to live on earth to be a servant, and it makes you more like him.

Next, let us talk about some bad things that happen to empty nesters. I have talked to several people who found themselves in this situation. The sad news is that some couples wait until now to get divorced, and when interviewed, say they were just waiting around for the last child to leave the house. The marriage is over, and they don't ever want to see that man or woman ever again for the rest of their life. Now that is some serious bad talk. I suppose the hatred for the mate in these cases takes a long time to fester and burst. It builds up in the one who wants the split and makes them feel cheated that they invested so much of themselves in all those years of marriage. The women in this position tend to feel like "He robbed my good years when I could have found someone else to love and now I am too old and no longer attractive, and my life is ruined."

Flip the situation and look at some of the men I have talked to who get into a relationship with a younger woman and are ditching the wife who raised their children for a new, younger, more attractive woman. Some women don't make enough effort to look good and dress up a little for their husbands when they come home. A lot of well-off professional men find someone who works for them to be available candidates for an affair, and a possible next wife. They sometimes don't realize they are being set up, at least to some extent.

In an article in the FactTank section of the Pew Research Center's website, Renee Stepler reveals statistics from the past 25 years that show age groups 25–39 had a -21-percent decline in divorces, age group 40–49 had a 14-percent increase, and the 50+ group (the so-called Baby Boomers) had a 109-percent increase, more than double the 1990 numbers, so Boomers are splitting up in record numbers. It is sometimes called the "Gray Divorce Revolution." Their research also noted that the main reason is that later-life divorcees have grown unsatisfied with their marriages over the years and are seeking opportunities to pursue their own interests and independence for their remaining years. The report also noted that divorce at this stage in life can also have some downsides. "Gray divorcees tend to be less financially secure than married and widowed adults, particularly among women."[1] So even though the idea may sound appealing on the surface, it really is a rather negative picture.

Can some of these marriages be saved? Definitely. Let us examine some major causes. Once they no longer have the kids to focus on, they find they have nothing in common. The Kids were the glue holding everything together, so one of the most constructive things to do is planning and scheduling that forces the couple to do things together and with other couples their age. Perhaps go on a cruise together or to a nearby resort for a weekend and spend time together. It is not essential but helps if they all go to the same church, eat out together, play golf, cards, board games, go to Branson, MO, for example or to a casino together, go to the movies, plays, or concerts, whatever everybody wants to do, whatever is appropriate for everybody. It strengthens all the marriages in

1. Pew Research Center, Stepler, "Boomers' Divorce Rates"

this group that "play and do things together" and makes life-long friends. People in these groups tend to forget ideas of divorcing because they are all having a fun time.

Doing things together can also involve doing charitable things that take at least two people, like Meals on Wheels or taking other meals to older or infirm people. My challenge to the empty nesters is to do things together. Take walks, go to the gym in bad or cold weather, and both of you exercise together, and get some other couples doing it also.

Some days, Carolyn and I would get in the car and find a country road we had never been on, and we would drive till we got totally lost and were laughing and joking that we must be in Tennessee by now, and finally find our way back to someplace we recognized. We discovered so many beautiful places that way, and then we would go home all aglow from having a nice time together, and all it cost was a little gas and an adventurous spirit. I told you earlier that we had something special in our relationship that a lot of our friends didn't. We didn't have to be entertained, we made our own by just being together. Try it, you'll like it.

Some of our best and most fun times were exploring old empty houses. Once after a tornado hit our town and its outskirts, we went driving around to look at the damage and found an old plantation house had been hit and the roof was blown off. There had been a lifetime of old papers and receipts stored in the attic. Otherwise, the house and property had been deserted for most of the Twentieth Century. The papers were scattered over several acres, so we picked up what we could to see if they revealed any clues about who had lived there. After finding the name of the original owner, we tried to contact his heirs and even contacted two local historians (who were no help). There were some interesting things like a receipt for thirteen pairs of shoes from mid-eighteen hundred, receipts for bulk orders of flour, sugar, and coffee beans, and a most interesting speech written in beautiful penmanship to be given at the dedication of the Missionary Ridge National Park near Chattanooga, following the Civil War. The speech rivals the Gettysburg Address. Its writer was one of the owners of the plantation and was a State Representative. You can have adventures wherever you go if you love and enjoy being with each other and make your own fun.

I am strongly suggesting you take day trips and explore your own area and you will find interesting things, wherever that happens to be. Take weekend getaways and several vacations each year and visit all over the States and Canada, which is a treasure just to our north. Quebec and Montreal are like a trip to Europe, and British Columbia has magnificent scenery. You can watch the Orcas play in the Sound and have High Tea at the Empress in Victoria. Then take the ferry back to the United States mainland. Do these kinds of things, and the word "divorce" will disappear from your vocabulary and never enter your mind. You should also remind yourselves, as you enjoy seeing other parts, of the world that God created all these beautiful things and places for our pleasure.

I have a circle of friends who do exactly what I have been saying. They are on the move continuously, sometime together, sometimes as couples, but they all take advantage of every opportunity to either see this country or spend time in Europe or elsewhere abroad on tours, cruises, or just sightseeing. They also own a variety of motorhomes, beach property, time shares, mountain and lake retreats, and all seem to enjoy them to the maximum. Our church has a group called the 39'ers, who go all over on buses and have a wonderful time together. Start your own group. Do something bold and join the crowd of empty nesters who are always on the move. Plan a trip with all your friends: start small and grow it into a habit.

In conclusion, empty nesters have the most potential to have a very good, fulfilling life well into old age, their travel is easier to manage, vacation locations cater to their needs, there are numerous opportunities for donating time to worthwhile charitable activities, and you can work at whatever makes you happy as long as you want. It can be the best years of your lives together. It is up to you. It takes compromise and willingness to do something you might not want to do once in a while, but do it anyway—you won't be sorry.

I am reminded of Billy Graham's seven principles of living, listed here with the scriptures that inspired them or are their basis.[2]

1. Make it your goal to live at peace with others. Romans 12:18
2. Treat others the way you'd want them to treat you. Matthew 7:12
3. Pray not only for your friends but for your enemies. Matthew 5:43–44
4. Guard your tongue. Psalm 141:3
5. Never repay evil with evil. Romans 12:17
6. Don't be a captive to the past. John 8:36
7. Practice the transforming power of forgiveness. Colossians 3:13

I think God endorses them without question. In a sense, if you always do Number 2, the others would pretty much take care of themselves. Our "Me first" society tends to change up the Golden Rule and it becomes "do unto others before they get a chance to do it to you.

2. Graham, *The Journey*, 211–14.

9

Retirement And Your Legacy

RETIREMENT IS BEST DONE when you don't want to go to work anymore ever. That is my definition. You have made up your mind to find other things to fill up your days. And that may be harder than you imagined. Assuming your wife is already not working at an 8:00 to 5:00 job but is running the house, your being there in the way may not be totally to her liking. Women take to retirement better than men. In a short while, retired men will want something to do, so some have already made big plans, and some say they want to have nothing to do and see how it feels. If this is the case, good luck, because you will get bored quickly. I'll give you two weeks and you'll be walking around looking for something to fix or maybe to tamper with, so you'll have to go to the home improvement store and buy parts. Once you have fixed everything around your house, you'll probably want to go fix everything for the kids. Well, this is noble work, but it will soon get old and you will need a better course of action. Are you tired of staying home already? Yep! Go to Wal-Mart and be a greeter, or better yet go to talk to the people that run your church and see what really isn't being done that you could perhaps take on as a project. You are suddenly now back in your element—working.

On the other hand, if you have a passion for something that you could never get to do because you worked too much, retirement may be just what you need. Make your bucket list and check it over and get on with it. Just hope your mate agrees with at least 80 percent of it and things will be okay most probably. Make sure you look at her bucket list, too. Agree to doing some of her ideas with her. Sharing everything will be the most important thing that keeps your marriage together until one of you dies.

One more word about sharing is that you both do not have to be doing the same things to share each other's enthusiasm for whatever either of you want to do. For example, if you want to make a leaded glass window, your wife doesn't have to lift a finger to help but needs to support your decision to make it. Together, you must develop a mutual respect for what the other wants or needs to do by themselves sometimes. Your wife may want to join a group who do quilting, so be happy for her. You two can be happy doing two totally opposite things and enjoying the relationships with others. Stay busy and have a list of many things you want to do eventually. In other words, build a backlog of things you both are looking forward to doing and add some charity efforts to the list, even one good thing you intend to do with some regularity. This will help you avoid periods of boredom and times when you miss working.

You really won't miss working as much as you think, but old habits die hard. You need to stay busy. Cultivate a few friends who also seem to be underutilizing their available free time and meet at least once a week for breakfast or lunch. Go to the library and pick up a couple of books by your favorite authors and read at least one per week. Encourage your spouse to go to the library with you. Borrow a movie from there occasionally.

Some of you may not feel it is time to retire, but if the company you work for has a mandatory retirement policy you do not have much choice, so you retire. But nothing keeps you from going to work for a different company that does similar work, unless you signed a non-compete statement (these usually have a time limit that expires in a reasonable time.) The point is that there are numerous opportunities to be hired, especially if you have specific skills, even after age 65. There are penalties for age discrimination in the workplace that give you some protection when seeking another job.

You have a lot of choices to continue to work if you really want or need to. I retired from a big aerospace company and decided I didn't want to stay home, so I became a consultant and part-time visiting professor to do teaching. I work just about the right amount and help three companies on an as-needed basis. It keeps me as busy as I want to be, and I actually have fun doing it most of the time. I believe it keeps people younger and sharper mentally to work at something that makes them get up in the morning, get dressed, get out, and appreciate another day.

Now is a good place to segue into talking to you about your legacy. It doesn't matter how much you have saved in your lifetime as much as it means to have a plan to distribute it fairly and with purpose to family members, your church, other charities, and perhaps someone or someplace where it is needed. So, one way to reduce your anxiety about who gets what and how much, you may want to distribute at least some of it before you die. This way, you can see how the recipients react, and feel that you have been able to share with them now at a time they need it most, rather than when you are gone. Some older people have the idea that all these things should remain a surprise until you die and your Will is read and I believe that is very wrong. You raised your children, so be as open and honest with them as possible and everyone will happier and better satisfied if you do.

My wife and I helped our kids when the time seemed right and funded 529 College Plans for our grandchildren. I also try to be generous at Christmas and times when special needs occur. We also give to various charities, both in our church and other places. There are so many needs you cannot possibly honor all the requests you get, so try to pick ones that have the best reputations. Unfortunately, after a couple years or so of giving to them, some may sell your name and address and you are deluged with requests from all over, so be careful to avoid this if possible.

I urge you to keep up with who gets what and try to be very fair about what you give away. That is why I suggest you and your mate make a formal plan and ask your executor to make sure your plan will be followed. I remind you that what you have in insurance and inheritable securities like IRAs and Brokerage accounts go to those written in the beneficiary statements and not your Will. Beneficiary statements trump the Will every time and let those assets avoid probate, so make sure they say what you want them to say. Pick the most reliable money manager in your family to be the executor. If you have a trust, pick your successor wisely as well, so that the property gets a fair distribution. Do not leave a bank in charge of your estate. They will charge exorbitant fees and my experiences have been very poor in their ability to manage investments and usually make a mess out of distributing assets like personal property of the deceased.

Most people probably do not need an estate planner per se; just make common sense decisions, write things down, and sit down with those who will inherit and explain your plan to them. However, if you have a large and complicated estate and you think you need professional help, then go to an estate planner. The lawyer who draws up your wills is usually not the person who is best suited to do estate planning. Find a person whose sole job is estate planning and get strong recommendations from others before investing any time and money. This is especially important if your children will inherit a lot of property and personal things of value, like jewelry, collections, antiques, rare coins and books, and things of sentimental value.

You should have a large durable 3-ring notebook, keep it where it can easily be found, show the place to your executor, and let him or her read it. Keep a copy of everything important in that notebook, including the Wills. Investment records should be in their own notebook and be kept up to date, and the executor should also know where that is kept. Nothing is more frustrating to the executor than to have trouble finding your important documents at a time of grieving. You might want to invite your children some weekend and ask them how they will divide your things. They usually have already talked about it among themselves, so solicit their inputs. It is a lot better to work some of these issues out before the parents die.

Before she died, Carolyn had made a box of things she treasured for each child in the family. It was incredibly touching to go through them and see what she had saved for each one as they grew up, married, and had their own children.

I think one of the nicest things you can do for your legacy when you are the surviving parent whose spouse has died, is to write something personal to each child and grandchild. These letters don't have to be long. Just tell them how much you love them, how proud you are of their accomplishments, what they mean to you. I don't want to suggest what you say because these things are quite personal, and you will figure it out when the time comes, but it may help them come to closure, which is sometimes very difficult, especially if there were any issues that were never settled during your lifetime.

You must remind yourself that God loves all his creation, something we humans have trouble doing. So, the more like Jesus we try to become, the more forgiving we must be. This translates into completely forgiving and forgetting any ill feelings against anyone in your life that offended or did you wrong or misjudged you in any way: past spouses, a child who has a grudge against you, the bully who beat you up in grammar school, the friend who turned against you when you were falsely accused and could have testified for you and didn't, the person at work who tried to set you up, the friend who stole your old girlfriend. You must make a complete clean sweep. Your forgiveness cleanses you just as it cleanses them, and makes you right with God, even if they don't know it. This is one of the most difficult concepts of salvation that people will face. Jesus took away our guilt on the cross, and we must pass along the favor and forgive those who we believe sinned against us.

Your legacy should be to leave this earth a little better place than had you never lived, to be faithful and loving to your spouse and children and grandchildren, to give them a fair distribution of your possessions, to be remembered by your friends as a good and faithful companion, and one who loved God unconditionally and found his purpose for you in this life.

10

Putting on the Whole Armor of God

You may have noticed the circles on the cover of the book. We are about to explore the fifth Life Circle. In earlier chapters, I alluded to a discussion of our spiritual life forces and it is here that we will explore what I believe is the greatest feature and asset of Life Circles. I want to start slowly to prove to you as we go along that the fifth circle is essential in your life. Without it, you won't be protected from forces that abound today, trying and succeeding in many instances to destroy the institution of marriage as well as our relationships in general. Look at the statistics. Never have so many people been divorced; never have so many people been so dissatisfied with their mates; and never have so many been unwilling to compromise and try to get along better. Europe is also having these problems, but not to the extent we find in the United States.

First, I want everyone to have a basic understanding of the fifth circle. Let's go back to and elaborate on what Jeff Walling defined as lukewarm Christians. These are the Sunday morning (plus perhaps Wednesday night) Christians who complain if the sermon is even a little too long, the music isn't the hymns they happen to like, the temperature isn't just right, the sound is poor, etc. They half-listen to the sermon, and they just don't get it. They really don't walk out the door inspired to have a better week than the last one, to do something nice for somebody, or to stay in the afterglow of a spiritual experience till they meet again. For some, it is a social event; for some, a mixer; for others, an obligation they need to satisfy. Down deep, they didn't enjoy the experience and they are on the outside looking in. They have not become a part of the core body of The Church. They can take Communion and not feel emotion that Jesus died on the cross giving his body and blood as a living sacrifice for our sins. Their Spiritual circle is like the one shown below. It crowds its way in wherever there is room—usually between the Family and Friends circles and sits there taking up time and space. It is too small to get a label in its circle, so I gave it an arrow.

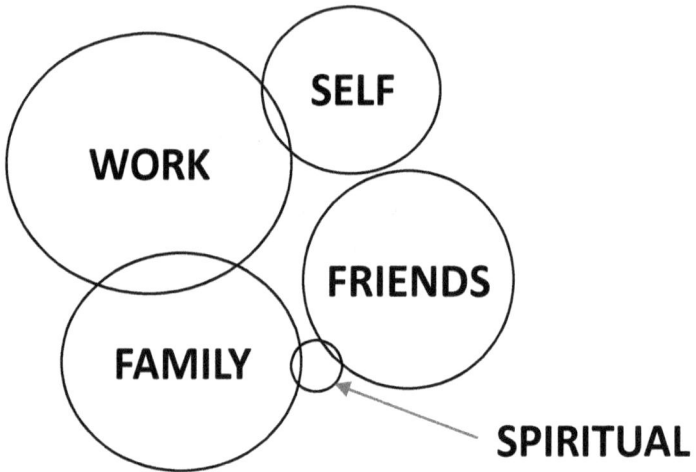

Figure 7. Putting all Your Life Circles Together

Yes, it is the fifth circle, but this is not the view I want to leave you with. That one is entirely different. A simple analogy addresses my point. I have a garden hose, like everyone who owns a house. Mine can supply one gallon of water every 15 seconds when the hose nozzle is turned on fully, but if I use a different setting that makes a fine mist, the hole is more restricted, much less water comes out, and it will take two minutes to fill the gallon bucket. The resistance created by a smaller nozzle aperture is like the resistance of the lukewarm believer. The water pressure remains the same, the hose hasn't changed, but the user has chosen a setting that greatly reduces the flow. Being lukewarm restricts your involvement to a couple of hours in the circle and then it disappears until the next time there is a church service you attend.

The full flow effect is present when we are baptized and come out of the water a new person, a Christian with a clean slate and a fresh start, with the indwelling of the Holy Spirit to guide us unimpeded by any resistance or restrictions, to help us do the right things in our lives and to super-charge our consciences. We are given a choice at this point: accept and believe and thus become strong believers or put up some resistance that diminishes the flow of all the good things associated with being one of God's chosen for everlasting life.

The ticket to heaven comes with a price. You must embrace it all. You can't pick and choose what you believe and accept. As hard as it is for some people to do this, it is the requirement. It is part of the price I just mentioned, Next, you must love God in the Three Persons with all your heart, soul, and mind and with your actions. With all these things, you discover what being faithful and righteous are all about, even though we mortals can never get there by ourselves. That is only possible by the Grace of God, paid for us by Jesus Christ, who took on our sins on the cross so that we could have everlasting life.

You cannot intellectualize your belief and try to do your own interpretations, which is what I tried to do when I was a young adult. You must study the Word, because that is where the answers lie, sometimes beneath the surface, other times right there in plain sight, but all the answers of how to live your life are there. I hope I convinced you.

Another simple analogy: You will never learn to swim if you stand knee deep in the water. You must get in all the way and sink first, then struggle some, and finally get in the rhythm of holding your breath and moving your limbs. In the beginning, it isn't easy, and you get choked sometimes, but eventually you master it. You will never appreciate God's Glory here on earth if you don't look up from your work and laugh and smile and enjoy every day as if it is your last.

Are you ready for the secret I promised from the beginning of the book? Shown next in Figure 8 is what happens to the Life Circles of the strong believer. The Spiritual circle surrounds your Work, Family, Friends, and Self circles. It does not require you to set aside hours for its circle. It is distributed across all your other four circles and permeates them and covers them. It becomes a way of life for all your endeavors. It protects you from outside forces that are in our lives more today than ever before in recorded history. It provides the glue that keeps families together. It will help you balance your work with your family's needs and your friendships will be stronger and more rewarding. It will protect you from temptations from the devil, which bombard us daily. The Spiritual Circle is the biggest of all because it surrounds our lives and protects us from needless divorce and inspires us to do better work, be nicer to everyone we meet, better parents and spouses, and a better friend.

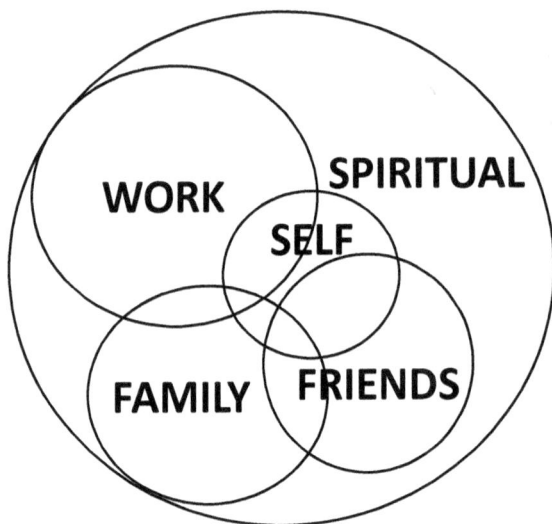

Figure 8. The Holy Spirit Protects All Your Life Circles

The Apostle Paul put it this way: "Finally, my brethren, be strong in the Lord and in the power of His might. Put on the whole armor of God, that you may be able to stand against the wiles of the devil." Eph 6:10–11. I urge you to continue reading through verse 20. In fact, all of Ephesians is a guide to how you need to live your life. It makes excellent reading. When we realize that it is God's own spirit that lives in us, then we should be much more selective in what we read, think, say, do, and watch on television and movies. This includes those with whom we associate. Realize also, the Spiritual circle protects all the other circles, including Work. I have been pleasantly surprised through the years how many people there are in the workplace who are strong believers. They invariably make the best work associates.

When I was growing up, my mother made some of the worst choices imaginable picking people for me to have as friends. Sometime, kids can sort those things out for themselves better than their parents. If there isn't the necessary chemistry between two acquaintances, then the parents should not push it. If you raise your children to be believers, discuss religion openly in the family, regularly attend worship services, and encourage them to be in the youth group, you have a very good chance they will be as strong members as you, and they will pick good friends because your friends are examples to go by. This is so important in today's skeptical society in which your peers may try to convince you that church is not nearly as much fun as what they have in mind.

Have you ever encountered a serious skeptic who claims to believe in God because something had to create all the universe, but they cannot grasp the idea that God is invisible to us here on earth and yet exists? They claim it isn't rational; they always want to know where he is. They argue that Heaven can't be somewhere above our heads in the sky. I like to ask them if I can give them something to ponder, and if they say yes, I ask them if they can see electricity? No! Can you smell it? No! Can you feel it? Yes, sometimes! Can you use it for benefit of mankind? Yes! Does it help you have a better life? Yes! My friend, you have just described some of the attributes of God. Various forms of electricity are everywhere we go in the clouds, in the air, in space, in huge magnetic fields surrounding the earth from pole to pole. Like electricity, God is everywhere. He is omnipotent and omniscient and omnipresent.

He spoke everything into being. He is timeless, the beginning and the end. Is it difficult to believe in God because he is not visible to us in this world? Is it so difficult for you to believe in other invisible things like wind, air, radio waves, and x-rays? All these things are invisible. If you strive to be like Jesus, and live as righteous a life as you can, you too can inherit the Kingdom of God wherever it is.

Some people still have their spiritual resistance turned up high and think they have all the required skills to make the important decisions in their lives on their own because they have always done it that way and it works out fine most of the time. They believe the worst fallacy of all, that they did it all on their own, and their egos begin to swell. Perhaps they don't realize that God gives them a lot of chances to get it right because he loves them as their father, which he is.

Earlier in this book, I refer to God as our autopilot. He can be if you let him. He can help you set the course your life should follow, but you must trust him by taking your hands off the controls and letting him drive you in the right direction when you might have picked another path: the one that looked more exciting and enticing, the one with whatever appeals to your carnal nature. I believe the Youth at our churches across America are some of the most important assets we have today to protect our churches in the future. As some young people turn away from even going to church, our youth seem energized to help in every way we ask. The figure below sums up the differences between the churched and the unchurched young unmarried in our society today. Believe me, I see it working and am proud of our youth.

The diagram below asks the question of young unmarried people to determine if they regularly attend church or not. Many churches today have Youth Groups that frequently do benevolent things for the shut-ins in the congregation and assist with Thanksgiving and Christmas food giveaway efforts, etc. Many of these young people make life-long friends at church. When they are baptized, they all have the indwelling of the Holy Spirit to be their "Autopilot." They tend to grow up strong in the faith and enjoy doing things to help people that need assistance. They are always willing to work at church when called upon. Almost all of them are very impressive in their Bible knowledge and most go on to college and do well in their careers. I see God working in their lives and am pleased to be a part of their support system. They renew my faith in the American life style.

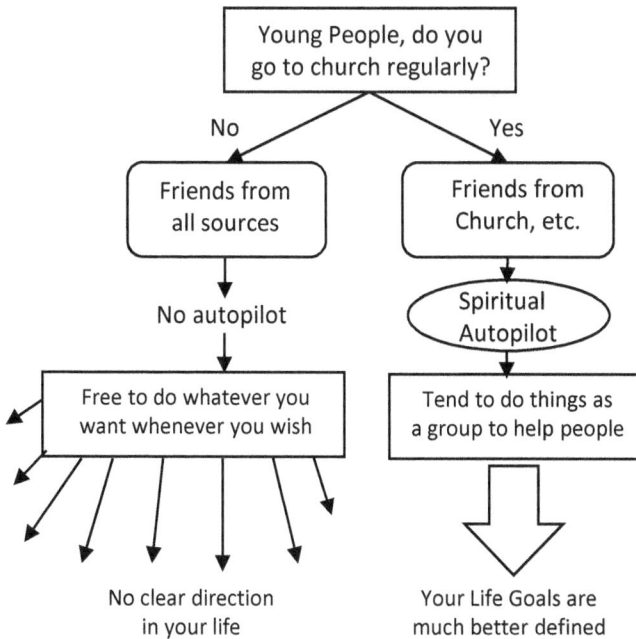

Figure 9. Churched and Unchurched Youth

The problems we all face as adults, male or female, young or old, is we think we can handle all the devil throws at us because we are smart, worldly, and perhaps even a little suspicious of things that seem too good to be true. But time and time again, we underestimate how clever the devil really is. He can cover up the temptations of this life in a beautiful wrapper sort of like a Christmas present that we are just dying to open to see what is inside. Both sexes are attracted to things that appeal to our senses, but that have little to do with following a more righteous path.

I discussed the conscience briefly, earlier in the book, relating how I felt my conscience had merged with the Holy Spirit in my life when I was growing up till about age 17, only to let that merger slip away when I became a young adult. Then I gave into temptations of all sorts, and it messed up my life for a rather long time. I ignored the Holy Spirit, who was my earlier autopilot, and gave into all sorts of things without fear of consequences, thinking I could handle every situation all by myself. When you ignore your conscience enough times, the little voice inside you gets weaker and weaker, and even though you may still possess the Holy Spirit and a conscience, you stop paying any attention to them. To become a more righteous person again, you need a day of reckoning when you finally convince yourself that you cannot manage your life all by yourself and that God is in control. You then confess to him and ask for forgiveness. He will hear you but remember getting back in God's better path will take some time and work on your part. You will have some bad habits to give up and will need a change of how you view your fellow man. You must listen and pay attention to that conscience of yours again.

Without the protection of the Spiritual Life Circle wrapped around us, we fall for the tricks of the senses. It looks great, smells great, sounds nice, feels smooth and soft, has all the appealing things that we like and admire. Is it a new sporty car that just seems perfect for me? It could be, but don't look at the price sticker because it will kill the deal right away; maybe think more about easy monthly payments. If it gets to be too much, you can always trade it in. So, you continue to be more enamored with it the more you look it over. You leave and come back several times and it looks better each time you see it, so you take it for a test run, and you notice a few things you don't like, but you can overcome them and they wouldn't bother you too much, so you overlook them and you want it really badly because it has some features that you just must have, that you never had before, or so you think. And therein lies your problem.

Your conscience kicks in and asks, *Was the old model you had worn out?*

No!

Did it have all the essential features the new model has?

Yes!

Why do you want this so badly?

I don't know, because it's new and exciting and my senses are urging me to close the deal.

Are you sure you can afford it?

Of course, with the easy payment plan they showed me.

What I just described is not a new car. Rather, it is a man or woman who just met someone who turned on all their senses and who said, "I need to be yours. Please take me home. I will be so much better than that older model you have now, and I am new and available on the easy payment plan. I will help you close the deal, so see me anytime you like while you are getting rid of the old model. I won't let you down. I love you already, yet I hardly know you. I know it's real and I am so excited too." It was lust at first sight.

At this point the buyer has a choice. He went for the test run and it was new and exciting but had a few things he didn't like, although mostly his senses were saying, "Do it. Close the deal. You deserve to be happy. It will all work out just fine." He must decide soon. What will he do? He has two obvious alternatives: If he lets his conscience and the Holy Spirit into the decision process, he will back out and soon realize how lucky he is. On the other hand, if he lets his senses and lust guide him, he will continue to think he is a big winner for a little while, but actually he becomes the big loser and will end up turning his life upside down as that payment plan he thought would be so easy will own him for many years to come. A lot of people take this path, and many have regrets for a long time after.

When you have been divorced for some time or your spouse dies, and you are looking for a new mate, these things only apply from the standpoint that you still must be guarded. You may be driven almost exclusively by your senses, which can mess you up very badly and very quickly. You really need to check the person out. Just how you do this is up to you to figure out but do not take their word for everything. You are facing a life-changing decision, so do not take it lightly. Here are my top 8 telltale indicators you may want to watch for that indicate things may not be what they should be: If a person scores high on this list, Look Out!

1. An inability to show you if they have debts, exactly how much they owe, on what, and for how long, because you will end up being responsible for them.

2. An inability to tell you in words how much they love you.

3. An inability to say what year they got their only divorce if they claim to have had only one and on what grounds it was granted.

4. You initiate almost every conversation when riding in the car for a couple of hours, and if you don't, he or she just sits there quietly, saying nothing.

5. Begins to voice a litany of things they don't like—food, styles, music, books, movies, sports, etc. instead of things they like. This is a negative thinker.

6. Doesn't want to cook for you or surprise you with little favors.

7. Doesn't like Christmas. This would be a deal breaker to me. I love Christmas!

8. Complains a lot about backaches, headaches, etc. A chronic complainer.

The last thing you need in another marriage is more problems than you have being single. So be careful what you wish for, because a new marriage brings its own set of baggage no matter how well you know the person, and there are always at least a few surprises. Seek legal advice and get a prenuptial agreement that protects both parties in the event of problems later. Even when your children want you to be happy and tell you so, they will still have some reservations until the new mate proves to be the fine upstanding person you thought you were marrying.

That first Christmas together will be a strong indicator of how your marriage will go in the future. If it flunks the test, you have a big problem that you may or may not be able to work through. If it goes very well, it can cement life-long relationships, so pray it does.

A new second or later marriage is a great experiment. In some ways, it is easier to "manage" than the first marriage, because both parties know a lot more about the intricacies than the true newlyweds, but by the same token, the first-timers have the energy and perseverance to work harder than the next-timers. I think I just invented a new term, "next-timers". Next-timers all too often have family issues to overcome and need to be dedicated to each other to get through these difficult negotiations. It takes a lot of love and kindness on everyone's part. Throughout this book, I have often urged next-timers to have a date night every week so that they can escape family pressures for a few hours and come back refreshed and loving. It is my recipe for any successful marriage, first, second, or whatever. Go out, have fun, and live it up a little, and thank God every day for each other and for your good fortune. Remember to love God with all your heart, soul, mind, and body and the rest should take care of itself if you made the right choice. Remember that all marriages, regardless of what number it is, require openness, continuous compromise, and sharing the work and responsibilities; they cannot work unless each person does his or her share.

In summary, leading a spirit-filled life regardless of your marital status—single, married, divorced—has so many rewards it is incomparable to a life with nothing to look forward to. It changes everything about your life and your expectation for heaven for the better. It makes you joyful to serve others, it makes you want to share your happiness, it enables you to see God's Glory in everything you do and everywhere you go. The Apostle Paul said it so much better:

"Finally Brothers, whatever is true, whatever is honorable, whatever is just, whatever is lovely, whatever is commendable, if there is any excellence, if there is anything worthy of praise, think about these things. What you have learned and received and heard and seen in me—practice these things, and the God of peace will be with you. Phil 4:8–9.

11

Time to Re-examine Your Life Circles and Re-Balance Your Life

By this time, you should understand your own Life Circles a lot better. You may have already realized you need to do something soon about an imbalance you noticed. You may or may not know what to do about it or how fast you need to correct it. The nature of it has a considerable influence on how fast it can be fixed.

The first step requires two things; look at the circles you drew when you began the book and then consult your list of original concerns. Underline the ones that are still concerns after reading the book. If you eliminated a few, that is good. If you added a few or even several, good. This shows progress. Do these two things, the circles and the list, continue to point to better defining your problems and offer some degree of enlightenment? Now, prioritize your list. Prioritizing should be based on several things:

- First, is it having a damaging effect on your marriage?

- Second, is it affecting your health and/or wellbeing?

- Third, is it about your job or the amount of time you commute?

- Fourth, any other troubling concerns.

An example of serious marriage woes would include you and your spouse having serious issues (possibly yelling, slamming doors, refusing to sleep together, letting anger boil over, etc.) over how much time you spend away from home and are never there when he/she needs you. Another would be if you and your spouse disagree all the time over the kids. Another is if your spouse has given you an ultimatum of some kind. Still another is if your spouse doesn't really want to talk about it. You may need a counselor. I prefer a Christian counselor. Ask your spouse to read this book in the meantime; it may help you to find some common ground that you can agree on. It may take a few weeks to get in to talk to a good counselor, because the good ones tend to stay busy. Additionally, they cannot always solve your problems if severe. They will then help you find different help quickly. Some kinds of issues need immediate attention and remedy, especially if violence or severe depression is involved.

Now to the less serious and somewhat longer-to-fix things, such as your job not being what you thought it would be. You feel you need out regardless of the reasons and you don't think it can be fixed by talking to the boss or management. You need to begin that arduous task of job hunting and interviewing. Good luck. At least in this case, your crucial issues revolve around the job and not major issues at home, which are usually harder to fix. Even harder to fix situations involve combined work and home problems in which the two tend to irritate each other. In any case, get moving. Don't put it off any longer. Get your problems out on the table and discuss them openly with your spouse while making sure the children are not listening. They can become badly upset if they think their parents are having problems. Children need to believe their home is their safe haven.

Are your issues spiritual in nature? Is your church or other religious affiliation not a good match for you or your family? Go visiting. It can be sort of fun because in a sense you are doing the interviewing. In Christianity in the United States today, there is a greater selection than ever before, what with nondenominational and interdenominational churches springing up all over, so shop around and when you find one that really suits you, join it regardless of the "brand." There is a great sameness in beliefs among the more popular Protestant churches. Finding a different place to worship may be the answer to your prayers. Make sure if you have children that it is a full-service church including a Youth group or licensed preschool, depending on the ages of your children. In our visiting around in Florida, my daughter and son-in-law joined a church that didn't have a Sunday school or building and met in a borrowed auditorium. That part is okay, but having been through a major church building program once, I know it will be a long while before a church like that with no facilities can operate smoothly and offer the nice-to-have amenities like classrooms and a baptistry. Remember, a church is how much of yourself you put into it. It is a family who all need to love each other and know how to get along. You must be involved and become a servant, and things will work out just fine. You will make good friends wherever you go.

The second step: By now you have the prioritized list of concerns that you feel are important and need action on your part. Here is where it gets to be a bit more challenging. I want you to redraw your Life Circles the way you think they should be, based on your Work circle and Family, Friends, and Self circles. Now compare these with the original ones. At this point you should see where problems exist and begin to make some decisions on changes you feel you must make to improve the harmony and balance in your life forces. Record the changes and why you made them. Changes should include any resolutions you are making to improve the balance of your Life Circles and to eliminate your bad habits. Then, please write a short explanation of these changes so you will remember them for a long while.

I want you to be able to sit down with your mate and explain the results to her (or him). It must, by now, be obvious to your mate that you are serious about changing your life and that of the family, and are willing to do whatever it takes to make things better. If one of your problems is drinking too much, stop altogether that day. If it is gambling of any kind, stop altogether that day. If it is anger management issues, seek help immediately. Whatever it is, you can begin to fix it immediately with God's help. Do not be ashamed if you need to join a support group or see a counselor. They can help you stand by your resolutions and help you to understand your cravings and get past periods of temptation.

The third step: This step should normally wait at least three months and not more than six to be performed. I hope you are happy with the results of these efforts. It is optional, but I would like to receive feedback from the readers of this book who took it to heart, rebalanced your Life Circles, and are willing to tell me how it worked out for you. I would greatly appreciate it, and God Bless you all.

"For God so loved the world that he gave his only begotten Son, that whoever believes in him should not perish but have everlasting life." John 3:16

Bibliography

Graham, Billy. The Journey: How to Live by Faith in an Uncertain World. Nashville: Thomas Nelson, 2006.

Stepler, Renee. *Led by Baby Boomers, divorce rates climb for America's 50+ population.* http://www.pewresearch.org/fact-tank/2017/03/09/led-by-baby-boomers-divorce-rates-climb-for-americas-50-population/ [retrieved March 12, 2019]

www.ingramcontent.com/pod-product-compliance
Lightning Source LLC
Chambersburg PA
CBHW070505090426
42735CB00012B/2677